THE Bruce Lee Code

HOW THE DRAGON

MASTERED BUSINESS,

CONFIDENCE & SUCCESS

THOMAS LEE

CAREER
PRESS

This edition first published in 2023 by Career Press,
an imprint of Red Wheel/Weiser, LLC
With offices at: 65 Parker Street, Suite 7, Newburyport, MA 01950
www.careerpress.com, www.redwheelweiser.com

ISBN: 978-1-63265-203-4

Library of Congress Cataloging-in-Publication Data

Names: Lee, Thomas, 1977- author.
Title: The Bruce Lee code : how The Dragon mastered business, confidence, and
    success / Thomas Lee.
Description: Newburyport, MA : Career Press, 2023. | Includes bibliographical
    references. | Summary: "This book focuses on the business strategies prevalent
    in Bruce Lee's life and teachings that helped unlock his full potential. His
    attention to brand is a major reason why he continues to influence pop culture
    today, and he was a pioneer, being one of the first Hollywood stars to start his
    own production company. To recharge America's creative and entrepreneurial
    swagger, we need to reexamine how Bruce Lee did what he did. The book draws
    upon interviews with Lee's family and friends and Lee's extensive writings,
    as well as interviews with CEOs and executives, academics, and experts on
    innovation, life coaching, and personal growth"-- Provided by publisher.
Identifiers: LCCN 2022050512 | ISBN 9781632652034 (paperback) | ISBN
    9781633412873 (kindle edition)
Subjects: LCSH: Lee, Bruce, 1940-1973--Influence. | Leadership. | Branding
    (Marketing) | Maturation (Psychology)
Classification: LCC HD57.7 .L438 2023 | DDC 658.4/092--dc23/eng/20221207
LC record available at https://lccn.loc.gov/2022050512

Cover design by Sky Peck Design
Cover image © Bruce Lee Enterprises, LLC.
The Bruce Lee name, image, likeness and all related indicia are intellectual
property of Bruce Lee Enterprises, LLC. All Rights Reserved
Chapters 4–6 opener illustrations © Martinus Sumbaji | Dreamstime.com
Interior by Timm Bryson, em em design, LLC
Typeset in Warnock Pro

Printed in the United States of America
IBI
10 9 8 7 6 5 4 3 2 1

THE Bruce Lee Code

To Brad, Melissa, and Allyson,
for your friendship and unwavering support
during these tumultuous past few years.

CONTENTS

ACKNOWLEDGMENTS

I want to thank Michael Pye, my editor at Career Press, and my agent John Willig for championing this book. Special thanks also goes to Shannon Lee, the Bruce Lee Foundation, the Chinese Historical Society of America in San Francisco, Jane Chin, Janice Lee, and Christopher Fong.

PREFACE: WE ARE BRUCE LEE

Bruce Lee's charisma and fighting skills have inspired countless people around the world, especially Asian-American boys looking for a representative hero in pop culture to emulate.

I was not one of them.

In fact, I wanted nothing to do with Bruce Lee. Growing up outside of Boston during the 1980s, I was the only Asian student in my class, the son of Chinese immigrants who once owned a laundry. Bruce Lee brought me nothing but shame and humiliation. Every day, at least one white student would scream mock Chinese at me and pantomime kicks and punches.

"Yo, Bruce!" they sneered. "Show us your moves! Hi-yah!"

It also didn't help that the man and I shared a last name. Although Lee is actually a pretty common name among both whites and Asians, bullies don't much care about things like that.

Over the next decades, I really didn't give Bruce Lee much thought. I became a fairly successful business journalist focused more on advancing my career than on worrying about race and prejudice. Then two things happened: Donald Trump became president and Covid-19 spread rapidly throughout the world.

Trump's America First policies made me feel unsafe. I felt I was once again an outsider who was not welcome in the only country I had ever called home. His belligerence toward China didn't help either, slapping tariffs on China and accusing the Chinese of stealing American jobs—just the sort of hostile rhetoric that has led to tragic consequences for Asian-Americans throughout history.

Covid-19 struck in late 2019; by March 2020, Trump was stubbornly calling it the "China Virus," referring to the pathogen's emergence in Wuhan, China. To make matters worse, he also suggested that China had deliberately created the pandemic, despite scant evidence. Not surprisingly, the number of hate crimes against Asian-Americans soared.[1] From San Francisco to New York, Asian-Americans suffered physical and verbal abuse from people who blamed them for the virus. It reached a point where I was too scared to ride the subway or even leave the house—not that there was anywhere to go because of the shut-downs.

One day, I called my friend Janice Lee to catch up. She was working with the Chinese Historical Society of America in San Francisco to create a museum exhibit about Bruce Lee. Although he was born in San Francisco's Chinatown in 1940, the city had apparently never properly honored one of the greatest martial artists who ever lived. No plaques, no street names, zilch. Los Angeles, Seattle, and Hong Kong had museums that focused on Lee. Even Mostar, a city in Bosnia and Herzegovina, had dedicated a statue to the man, though he had never set foot there.

But Janice had another motive besides memorializing Lee. Asian-Americans really needed a hero they could rally around, she said. The community was so demoralized by Covid-19 and the resulting racist reaction that she thought an exhibit dedicated to Lee could lift spirits.

Although I had never been a huge Bruce Lee fan, given the context, the project intrigued me. I had never fully appreciated just how popular the man was and continues to be since his death in 1973, not just with Asian-Americans, but with, well, *everybody*—Blacks, whites, Latinos, male, female, old, young, athletes, musicians, actors— both in America and in the rest of the world. Like Muhammad Ali, the Beatles, and Martin Luther King Jr., Lee was one of the rare figures who transcended geography, race, and time.

I felt ashamed that I had avoided being associated with Lee as a young child. But that's what racism does; it distorts our sense of identity to the point that we reject the very people we would naturally admire and emulate. The proposed exhibit offered me a unique opportunity to right those wrongs, so I signed up as editorial director. But I wanted to do something different.

Museums normally organized Lee's life chronologically. While a perfectly sound approach, this just didn't seem to rise to the moment. The world was really hurting and we wanted people to find something in Lee's life that could inspire them. So we looked for ways to make his legend something to which people could relate.

Bruce Lee, after all, was perfectly human. Despite his almost supernatural physical skills, he failed for most of his life before he succeeded. He was hot-tempered and made plenty of mistakes. "And guess what," his daughter Shannon points out. "Bruce Lee himself was not good at a lot of things. He could barely change a light bulb or cook an egg."[2]

"To me, the function and duty of a quality human being is the sincere and honest development of one's potential."

But Lee deeply wanted people to realize their fullest potential—not by copying him (there is only one Bruce Lee, after all), but by applying his life's experience to their own situation. "Bruce Lee doesn't want me to be Bruce Lee," Shannon claims in *Be Water, My Friend*.

> What Bruce Lee wants is for you to be the best possible version of you that you can be. And that will look entirely different from Bruce Lee because, well, you are you.
>
> His words should encourage you to consider a process of self-actualization whereby you take a look at who you may actually and essentially be—where you notice what your potential is pulling you toward and how to work to cultivate that.[3]

People most often think of Bruce Lee as just a martial artist or an actor. But when you examine his life carefully, you find that four distinct personas emerge: the visionary, the athlete, the thinker, and the unifier. By harmoniously working together, these personas helped him to become the icon we know today.

As the visionary, Lee was always about the "big picture." He wanted to unite East and West, and he used martial arts as a platform to promote Chinese art and philosophy to global audiences. From blockbuster films like *The Big Boss* and *Way of the Dragon* to productions like *Fist of Fury* and *Enter the Dragon*, his movies fused the kinetic excitement of Hong Kong action movies with the character-driven narratives of prestige Hollywood and European cinema.

As the athlete, Lee was the quintessential martial artist, whether spinning high kicks or executing lightning-fast punches. In order to coax these performances out of his body, he spent an enormous amount of time researching health and nutrition, focusing specifically on strength as a way to increase speed and flexibility. The result was a body that graced the pages of physical-fitness magazines around the world.

As the thinker, Lee paid equal attention to cultivating his mind. He read and wrote extensively about the works of both Eastern and Western philosophers ranging from Carl Jung and René

Descartes to Zhuang Zhou and Jiddu Krishnamurti. He even developed his own martial arts philosophy called *jeet kune do*.

As the unifier, Lee's career coincided with the great social and political changes that swept the United States and the world during the late 1960s and early 1970s. While he did not actively campaign on social issues, he led by example, surrounding himself with people of all races and genders. His films, which feature characters who fight against systems of oppression, particularly resonated with African-Americans still struggling to overcome the legacy of slavery and Jim Crow.

It was these four personas that guided us as we created the *We Are Bruce Lee* exhibit in San Francisco's Chinatown. Our hope was that people could find their own inner Bruce Lee by examining the characteristics that had made this man so unique and special.

And that is how this book came about. While working on the exhibit, I noticed that Bruce Lee meant different things to different people. Some recalled the charismatic and attractive movie star who emerged at a time when Hollywood depicted Asian-American men as sexless or cartoonish. Others saw him as the symbol of Asian-American resistance against racism. Many just enjoyed him as the supremely talented entertainer he was.

But what about Bruce Lee the businessman? That may seem like a stretch. He studied philosophy and drama, never worked at an office job, and didn't demonstrate any particular interest in generating wealth. In fact, he wasn't even comfortable running his own personal business affairs. As Doug Palmer, a friend and former student, recalled:

> He was certainly savvy, but I think he knew his limitations too. And he realized that he would have to depend on somebody to look at the financial side of things. He also realized that there were people coming out of the woodwork who were trying to sell him this or that or get him to do this or that.

Palmer first met Lee in Seattle as a teenager, when the unknown martial artist was starting to attract local attention with public demonstrations of *wing chun*, a form of Chinese kung fu. He took classes with Lee and the two struck up a friendship before Palmer left for college. After earning a law degree from Harvard, Palmer went to work for a firm in Tokyo representing American companies operating in Japan. By then, Palmer hadn't spoken to Lee in several years, but he kept tabs on his former teacher's meteoric career.

Lee, the Entrepreneur

In 1969, after a disappointing career in Hollywood, Lee relocated to Hong Kong and, over the next few years, starred in a string of box office hits including *The Big Boss*, *Fist of Fury*, and *Way of the Dragon*. Lee's success made him a gigantic movie star in Hong Kong, where reporters and fans followed him wherever he went. But celebrity and money made him uneasy and he worried about whom he could trust.

In the fall of 1972, Palmer visited Lee in Hong Kong, just after he had finished filming his masterpiece, *Enter the Dragon,* and had moved on to shooting *Game of Death.* Palmer describes the reunion like this:

> We took him out to dinner and it was obvious that he was well known in Hong Kong because when we stopped in a taxi cab at a light, cars next to us would gawk. And when we walked into the restaurant, he was immediately given a table, even though the place was filled up.
>
> We talked about the possibility that I might, after I finished up in Japan, be interested in coming down to Hong Kong and helping with his business affairs, sorting through it all and trying to figure out whom he could trust and whom he couldn't. I think he realized that it would be helpful to have someone looking out for his back.

But business acumen is not just about running numbers or even about making money. When he joined his friend in Hong Kong, Palmer learned that Lee was an entrepreneur at heart, a man blessed with vision, tenacity, and curiosity. He wanted to spread the art and philosophy of kung fu to the West, first through schools and demonstrations, and then through mass media in the form of cinematic entertainment.

Bruce was entrepreneurial in the sense of making his own way and doing things his way and doing them on his own. But his interests were less financial and more toward the martial arts and later the movies that he was interested in getting out there.

I never got the impression that making money was his goal or was a major focus of what he was interested in. He was interested in money as a means of feeding his family and a means of keeping track of things and knowing that he was getting respect because, if he had respect, people would pay him.

Martial arts and kung fu in particular and developing his brand of it was one of the major thrusts of his life. And he saw the movies as a means of spreading his vision of what martial arts should be and could be. I think they complemented each other very well.

Given my long career as a business journalist (I was a columnist at the *San Francisco Chronicle*), I couldn't help but see Bruce Lee as a remarkable businessman and entrepreneur. Throughout his life, he demonstrated the kind of vision, creativity, and resilience that we celebrate in people like Steve Jobs, Elon Musk, and Bill Gates.

"Do not allow negative thoughts to enter your mind for they are the weeds that strangle confidence."

Lee's beliefs on innovation and adaptability are certainly relevant to the business community. And most important, he wasn't a just a talker or a thinker. He *did* things. He co-founded Concord Production so he could wield greater artistic and financial control over his film projects, which were enormously profitable. He started schools in Seattle, Oakland, and Los Angeles to promote his unique version of martial arts. And he was keenly aware of the power of his personal brand and actively explored merchandising deals before his death.

Today, Bruce Lee is one of the world's most valuable brands. He has inspired multi-billion dollar properties in comic books, professional mixed martial arts, music, fashion, and, of course, movies and television shows.

Lee's enduring popularity means that people have written and spoken about his impact as both a martial artist and a general self-help guru. Lee Huang, a former executive with NBCUniversal, Barnes & Noble, and Billboard, has led workshops across the country teaching executives how to use Lee's example to jump-start their own innovation programs. According to Huang:

> Every ethnic group, every demographic loves Bruce Lee. You can't really say that about any other global icon. Bruce Lee is a universally

loved figure. So all of his innovations, from JKD and health and fitness to his movies and bringing martial arts to non-Chinese folks, creating the brand of strong Asian men, translated into amazing business.

Lee's accomplishments as a visionary entrepreneur deserve more attention—especially during these tumultuous times. My goal in this book is to encourage readers to appreciate him fully as the savvy businessman that he was by applying modern-day business concepts and case studies to his career.

To that end, I have interviewed Lee's family and friends, along with executives and entrepreneurs who admire him. I have also relied extensively on his own words and writings, including letters, media interviews, and other documents. I hope the result is a book that will present Bruce Lee as the gifted entrepreneur that he was.

INTRODUCTION

Enter the Dragon

When Bruce Lee arrived in the United States from Hong Kong in 1959, he was a teenager without money, connections, or credentials. "Now I'm really on my own," he wrote to an aquaintence. "Since the day I stepped onto this country, I didn't spend any money from my father. Now I am working as a waiter for a part-time job after school. I'm telling you, it's tough, boy! I always have a heck of a time!"[1]

But what Lee did possess was a startlingly clear grasp of American capitalism and its potential for economic mobility. In 1962, in a letter to Pearl Tso, a family friend, about his impressions of his new home, he wrote:

Fortune, in the sense of wealth, is the reward of
the man who can think of something that hasn't
been thought of before. In every industry, in every
profession, ideas are what America is looking for.[2]

Although he was only twenty-one at the time, he
felt the vibrance of a nation that had emerged as
an economic and military superpower thanks to
its victory in World War II and the resulting economic boom of the decade that followed.

It was as if Lee were already starting to formulate
the beginnings of his own Horatio Alger story—a
man who succeeds in America through hard work,
ingeniuity, and ambition. "He's feeling the sense
of America," Shannon Lee said during one of her
podcasts. "He's very observant and picked up the
energy of America as an outsider."

In his letter to Tso, he writes:

I feel I have this great creative and spiritual force
within me that is greater than faith, greater than
ambition, greater than vision. It is all these combined. My brain becomes magnetized with this
dominating force which I hold in my hand.

When you drop a pebble into a pool of water, the pebble starts a series of ripples that expand until they encompass the whole pool. This is exactly what will happen when I give my ideas a definite plan of action. Right now, I can project my thoughts into the future, I can see ahead of me. I dream . . .

Whether it is the God-head or not, I feel this great force, this untapped power, this dynamic something within me. This feeling defies description, and [there is] no experience with which this feeling may be compared. It is something like a strong emotion mixed with faith, but a lot stronger.[3]

You can't help but be inspired by this—or, at the very least, root for his success.

Lee would later imbue his movie roles with that same charisma and inevitability, to the point that it is sometimes difficult to seperate the man from his art. He clearly feels as if he's someone on a mission, that he's destined to do something great in America.

Unfortunately, however, the America that Lee observed in 1962 is not the America we live in today. Although the United States still commands the largest and most technologically advanced economy in the world, the country has been experiencing a profound slump in confidence and creativity. That may sound surprising, given the breadth of the successful companies that call America home, including Apple, Google, Tesla, and Amazon. But the numbers don't lie.

Since 2000, the United States has experienced three disastrous recessions—the tech bubble, the housing crisis, and shut-downs that have severely dislocated the labor force and destroyed trillions of dollars in wealth. At the same time, productivity growth—the measure of output per worker—has been alarmingly weak, despite the emergence of technological advances like the Internet and artificial intelligence.

"Ideas have made America what she is.
A done good idea will make a man
what he wants to be."

Since 2005, labor productivity has grown at an average annual rate of just 1.3 percent, according to a report by the US Bureau of Labor Statistics (BLS).

From 2010 to 2018, labor productivity increased just 0.8 percent. The BLS estimates that the slowdown in productivity has cost non-farm businesses during this period a staggering $10.9 trillion or about $95,000 per worker.

> The productivity slowdown has been one of the most consequential economic phenomena of the last two decades … which has the effect of placing downward pressure on economic growth, worker compensation gains, profits growth, and gains in living standards of Americans.

Innovation, R & D, and the Workforce

Economists have been struggling to explain the source of the problem. One theory is that our innovation, the historical hallmark of US economic growth, has not been meaningful enough to boost the economy as a whole. In 2021, the United States fell out of the top ten of the world's most innovative countries, according to the annual Bloomberg Innovation Index, which measures things like research-and-development (R & D) spending, manufacturing capability, and concentration of high-tech public companies.[4] According to a BLS report:

> Businesses that have been spurring recent innovations are having difficulty expanding, and thus, their innovations are failing to make a bigger impact on the economy as a whole than would otherwise be the case. Many of the firms that have been innovating have not similarly been able to scale up and hire more employees commensurate with their improved productivity.

Moreover, the quality of US corporate R & D has been on the wane for several decades now. From 2005 to 2015, business R & D spending soared 78 percent to $355 billion, according to the National Science Foundation's National Center for Science and Engineering. Yet research shows that companies are not getting as much bang for their bucks as they should.

When Anne Marie Knott, a professor of strategy at Washington University's Olin School of Business in St. Louis, analyzed the performance of publicly traded companies since 1972, measuring productivity by comparing increases in R & D spending with increases in annual revenue, she found that corporate returns on R & D spending actually *declined* 65 percent. "This not only hurts companies and their stakeholders; it hurts the entire economy, because R & D is the primary driver of economic growth," she claims.[5]

Research also suggests that the US economy is not properly taking advantage of its diverse workforce. Despite women being far more educated than men, for example, the latter continue to dominate leadership roles and highly skilled professions like engineering, medicine, and finance.[6] As a result, companies and industries are still operating under business models developed years ago by white males.

Moreover, research has also shown that greater participation of women in the labor force produces wage gains for everyone.[7] For every 10-percent increase in women working, overall wages rise about 5 percent. Another study by S & P Global showed that firms with female CEOs and CFOs have produced superior stock-price performance compared to the market average.[8] In two years on the job, female CEOs oversaw a 20-percent increase in the stock prices of their companies and female CFOs witnessed a 6-percent increase in profits and an 8-percent jump in stock returns. And yet, men continue to dominate the ranks of CEOs, boards, and top management positions.

Immigration has always been key to America's economic success. And yet, the United States has cut the number of visas that highly skilled workers need to work and study in the country.[9] Bottom line: We're not getting the right workers to do the right jobs for our economy to reach its potential. We need energy and creativity from diverse voices, especially at the top. But the status quo stands firm.

And this was all *before* the shutdowns that severely disrupted not only the economy, but daily aspects of life that we took for granted—travel, going to the movies, getting the kids to school. The result is a shell-shocked country just stumbling about, seeking to hold on instead of reaching for the next big thing. We argue over who gets the biggest slice of the pie without trying to bake a bigger pie.

About seven in ten Americans think the economic system is unfair and generally favors powerful special interests, according to a poll by the Pew Research Center.[10] A majority believe that the economy is helping the wealthy and hurting the poor and middle-class. And roughly half of Americans say that the economy is hurting them and their families. Another Pew poll found that 49 percent of Americans think the availability of affordable housing in their local communities is a major problem, up ten percentage points from early 2018.[11]

The American dream seems increasingly like a vague memory.

More Bruce Lee, Please

Now, more than ever, we need Bruce Lee. Not to thrill us or entertain us, but to inspire us to meet our potential. He is, in fact, the epitome of the American dream. Despite the obstacles he faced (and there were plenty), the man who called both Asia and America home was able to fuse together the best of both worlds into a life and a legacy that continues to capture the imaginations of people around the world, regardless of race, gender, religion, or nationality. So much so that, to some, his name has become a verb of sorts—two words that together mean digging deep within ourselves and attacking challenges without fear or regret.

Perry Yung, who plays Father Jun in the HBO Max series *Warrior*, a show based on a Western kung fu idea developed by Bruce Lee, recalls preparing for his audition:

> I only got three days to memorize these lines. So, I'm working on it, I got to memorize it, I think I got it pretty good. The day of the audition comes. I'm meditating in the morning, I'm letting everything go, so that when the time comes, it's just all there, right? In a really clean way.

And then that morning, my partner goes: "Aren't you going to go to our son's orientation for high school today, this morning?" I had forgotten all about that.

Yung took his son to the event, which ended at noon, and then rushed to his audition an hour later. For actors, auditioning in front of casting directors is hard enough, but Yung was also flustered and stressed because he had messed up his schedule.

And I do the monologue, and I think I did pretty good, and then she cuts the camera and she goes: "Okay, just stop what you're doing. They want somebody really solid. Do you want to try it again?"

Yung's heart sank. He thought he had blown his chance.

But then suddenly, in a meta moment, Yung recalled the man who had inspired the series for which he was auditioning. "This is my moment," he said to himself. "This is Bruce. I got to channel Bruce." He rose to the moment and got the role.

Bruce's spirit couldn't be more relevant in today's troubled world, which is struggling to adjust to up-ended traditional structures and revised expectations about work and life. In the second half of 2021, more than 20 million people quit their jobs, including a record 4.4 million in September alone.[12] Employees between thirty and forty years old had the greatest increase in resignation rates, with an average increase of more than 20 percent between 2020 and 2021.

Steve Cadigan, a former top executive at LinkedIn, observes that these disruptions have prompted employees to question traditional assumptions about work and career. They have taught people that life is short and precarious, so perhaps working forty hours a week in a soul-crushing office may not be the best use of their time. If there was ever a time for people to ressurect their life's dream or seek out new opportunities, it may be now, Cadigan argues.

The world's changing faster now than it ever has before. We already are seeing more people make pivots, not just job changes, but career pivot changes to different sectors, different places. People are realizing: "I can see more places I can go, things I can do and places where I can work than ever. I want to try new stuff."

No one knew this better than Bruce Lee.

Lee's lifelong goal was to promote Chinese art and culture, particularly kung fu, in the West. At first, he thought he could do this by opening martial arts schools. But he soon realized that television and film could accomplish his mission much faster and more effectively. It is easy to take Lee's success and stardom for granted, but he had to overcome many difficulties and hardships in his life, most notably institutionalized racism. In fact, he only found success in Hong Kong after largely washing out in Hollywood. As Cadigan notes:

> There are so many domains where you can trip on something or come across something that

you can go all in on and you owe it to yourself to be experimenting and tasting and doing these things. And that's why I love Bruce Lee's story.

And what's amazing is that Lee didn't even have the technology that people enjoy today. Thanks to social media, people can instantly promote their work and develop their own unique personal brands.

"Remember that practical
dreamers never quit."

Given Bruce Lee's charisma, martial arts background, and philosophical musings, it's no surprise that he has evolved into his own self-help cottage industry. But viewing him through the lens of an entrepreneur and businessman offers valuable lessons that are uniquely suited for America and the world it currently faces.

President Calvin Coolidge is often credited with the famous quote: "The business of America is business." In reality, however, that's not exactly what

Coolidge said. Speaking to the American Society of Newspaper Editors in 1925, he remarked:

> After all, the chief business of the American people is business. They are profoundly concerned with producing, buying, selling, investing, and prospering in the world. I am strongly of the opinion that the great majority of people will always find these are moving impulses of our life.[13]

The quote earned Coolidge an unfortunate reputation as a pro-market laissez-faire hawk interested in nothing but greed and materialism. But Coolidge saw capitalism as a means to accomplishing great things—as the means to an end, not the end itself. In the same speech, he also said this:

> It is only those who do not understand our people, who believe our national life is entirely absorbed by material motives. We make no concealment of the fact that we want wealth, but there are many other things we want much more. We want peace and honor, and that charity which is so strong an

element of all civilization. The chief ideal of the American people is idealism.[14]

Bruce Lee understood this perfectly. He wanted to do great things. In fact, he believed all humans had a moral duty to achieve their full potential.

Lee was not naïve. He knew that America was a capitalist, market-driven country. But he also understood that it was a land that valued good ideas and acknowledged that financial success could turn those good ideas into reality. As he wrote to Pearl Tso:

> All in all, the goal of my planning and doing is to find the true meaning in life—peace of mind. I know that the sum of all possessions I mentioned does not necessarily add up to peace of mind; however, it can be if I devote [my energy] to real accomplishment of self rather than neurotic combat.[15]

The purpose of this book is to inspire entrepreneurs, the kind of people who have made America such a prosperous nation. I want to recapture their energy, their purpose, their creativity, and their grit by encouraging them to emulate, not just the words of Bruce Lee, but also his actions.

Bruce Lee was only thirty-two when he died tragically in 1973. But he lived several lifetimes over during his short time on Earth. In this book's first chapter, I present an overview of his inspiring life. In the remaining chapters, we will examine his life and his words through the lens of concepts critical to any entrepreneur's success—vision, innovation, adaptation, resiliency, curiosity, and branding. You'll also learn, through testimonials from entrepreneurs who describe in their own words why Bruce Lee means so much to them, just how much impact he has had on their lives. I hope what you read here inspires you follow in his footsteps.

CHAPTER 1

An Unmistakable Presence

Bruce Lee was born in San Francisco in 1940 then returned to Hong Kong with his family. Growing up in Hong Kong, he often found himself in pitched street fights with other boys, which prompted him to learn martial arts. At sixteen, he trained with wing chun master, Ip Man. He later moved back to the United States and studied philosophy at the University of Washington in Seattle. During this time, Lee started to gain notice with his exhibitions and classes on kung fu.

Doug Palmer, a student who later became a good friend, describes his early impressions of the martial art:

At the time, I was really into boxing because of its practicalness and usefulness. But in boxing, at least in the ring, there are a lot of rules. And you're not allowed to strike with anything but your fists. And when I saw kung fu, I realized it was a fighting system where you used not only your fists but your elbows, your feet, your knees, everything. It was designed to be the most effective way to deal with whoever you had to deal with in a physical confrontation.

In 1964, Lee opened his own martial arts studio in Oakland, California. Despite the disapproval of some Chinese there, he taught kung fu to anyone who wanted to learn, regardless of race, gender, or ethnicity.

That same year, Lee attended a karate tournament in Long Beach, California, where he demonstrated several martial arts moves, including his famous one-inch punch and two-finger pushups. Lee's electric performances caught the notice of Hollywood television producer William Dozier, who cast him in *The Green Hornet,* a series that followed the adventures of media mogul Britt Reid, who masqueraded as the eponymous masked vigilante. With his martial arts expert sidekick Kato, played by Lee, the duo battled crime throughout the city. Though it only ran for one season, the series introduced martial arts, and specifically kung fu, to millions of Americans, who were mesmerized by Lee's speed and seemingly superhuman physical abilities.

For Asian-Americans, however, Lee's role held a deeper meaning. For the first time, they saw someone who looked like them playing a major role on a big television show. And unlike previous depictions of Asians, which had shown them as weak and silly, Kato was a sleek, strong character who regularly defeated the bad guys.

Unfortunately, *The Green Hornet* was a frustrating experience for Lee. Although Kato was perhaps the most popular figure on the show, producers and writers didn't give him many speaking lines. Worse yet, his salary was equivalent to that of a stuntman, far less than the salaries of his fellow co-stars. After the cancelation of the series, Lee found a few small roles here and there, including in productions like *Marlowe, Here Comes the Bride,* and *Longstreet,* but Hollywood success largely eluded him. For all of his magnetism and physical skills, Lee could not overcome the institutional racism that dominated American movies and television. In particular, studios believed that his accented English would alienate audiences.

In truth, white-dominated Hollywood had long believed that Asian-American actors couldn't headline major films and television series, especially as romantic leads. Instead, they cast caucasian actors in Asian roles, a practice known as "yellowface" (see chapter 4). For example, Lee had discussions with Warner Bros. about starring in the series *Kung Fu,* a story about a Chinese Shaolin monk who travels the American Old West searching for his brother. The studio ultimately cast David Carradine, a white actor with no martial arts experience, in the role. Frustrated, Lee sought to revive his film career in

Hong Kong, hoping that Hollywood would take notice of his success.

Lee proved correct.

"Success comes to those who become success-conscious. If you don't aim at an object, how the heck on earth do you think you can get it?"

FROM HOLLYWOOD TO HONG KONG

Movie audiences around the world had never before seen the likes of Bruce Lee—the raw physicality, the blazing speed, the jumps, punches, and kicks that seemed to defy the laws of physics. Yet Lee, a champion ballroom dancer, infused his moves with unmistakable elegance and grace.

But Lee also commanded the screen with his charisma. His unmistakable presence drew audiences to him. His goods looks, remarkable body, and fighting skills up-ended historical stereotypes of Asian men as weak, passive, and sexless.

Lee's Hong Kong films were highly successful—and highly profitable. Beginning with *Big Boss*, his five films together grossed $3.1 billion against a combined budget of only $2 million (both figures adjusted for inflation; see chapter 3).

Enter the Dragon, widely considered one of the greatest martial arts films of all time, was a blockbuster even before Hollywood coined the term. When Warner Bros. released the film in the United States, the movie eventually topped the box office for two weeks straight, remained in the Top 10 for another four weeks, and hit #1 again in its eighth week. The film ultimately grossed $1.2 billion against a budget of just $850,000 (figures adjusted for inflation).

Bruce Lee's stardom in Hong Kong rivaled that of James Dean and the Beatles in the West. He hung out with celebrities like Steve McQueen, James Coburn, and Kareem Abdul-Jabbar. Photographers and reporters followed him wherever he went. His martial arts reputation prompted strangers, including one cab driver, to challenge him to fights.

Sadly, Bruce Lee died in 1973 at the age of only thirty-two. Ironically, he never got a chance to experience the success of *Enter the Dragon*, through which he posthumously realized his lifetime goal of worldwide stardom.

_____

"Don't fear failure.
Not failure, but low aim,
is the crime. In great attempts,
it is glorious even to fail."

_____

CHAPTER 2

A Man with a Plan

Bruce Lee and the Beatles were both pop-culture icons at the peak of their powers in the late 1960s and early 1970s. They both transformed their respective industries and enjoyed global popularity during a period of great socio-political turmoil. Unfortunately, they never met. But can you imagine such a meeting? The conversation would have been historic and the photographs epic.

And the Fab Four and the Little Dragon had something else in common as well. Despite never having graduated from a university, they were all blessed with incredible intuition that allowed them to perceive and understand concepts without knowing the actual vocabulary. John, Paul, George, and Ringo never had any formal musical training. In fact, none of them knew how to read or write music. During their early days in Liverpool, John and Paul frequently hopped on buses and traveled throughout the city to meet people just to learn new guitar chords. John Lennon once said: "I consider myself a primitive musician just because I never studied music."[1]

Producer George Martin, who was musically trained, often acted as the Beatles' "translator," refining their ideas and plugging the gaps in the band's musical knowledge. Yet the Beatles did just fine for themselves, producing some of the most innovative and successful songs in rock-and-roll history. The band may not have known the exact *vocabulary* of music theory, but they certainly understood the *substance* of music theory.

David Bennett, a musician who hosts a popular Internet show on music theory, argues:

Many people claim that because the Beatles didn't know music theory in any great depth, that analyzing their music is arbitrary, looking for meaning which isn't there, looking for intent which isn't there. But that misses the point on why we analyze songs. One of the things that music theory is useful for is as a set of tools to look under the hood.

I've heard time and again why music theory is just rules, that music theory limits creativity. But this couldn't be further from the truth. Music theory is a way of describing what there is to be used. If you don't know music theory and you don't know how to use it, then your songwriting and your musicianship is probably stuck in a box . . . But if you can know how to break out of that, then it opens up a whole well of possibilities.[2]

Bennett's argument also applies to business. You don't need an MBA and you don't have to speak an official vocabulary to run a business. Indeed, entrepreneurs like Steve Jobs and Richard Branson never completed college. As Jobs once said:

I readily understand that there are many things in life I don't have the faintest idea of what I'm talking about. Some mistakes will be made. That's good. Because at least that means some decisions are being made along the way.[3]

And yet knowing some theory—or intuiting it—can provide valuable insight into why certain people succeed and some don't. It certainly can't hurt.

We can reverse engineer people's careers to see how they demonstrated the best practices of starting and growing a business, whether they realized it or not. We can identify the tools necessary to unlock our creativity and take our businesses or careers to the next level.

And we can use business theory to "look under the hood" of the most famous martial artist and most underrated entrepreneur of his time.

LEE'S NORTH STAR

Bruce Lee was a man of incredible charisma and effortless appeal. But beneath these intangibles, he had the ability to stay focused on his North

Star—his dream of fusing the cultures of East and West into a successful business enterprise. To do this, he identified and followed three fundamental principles that he felt were necessary for a successful business: vision, strategy, and tactics. Let's quickly review the definition of each term, as people often confuse them. Then we'll look at how Lee applied vision, strategy, and tactics to his own business enterprises.

"At this point, I really don't know where the limit lies. I find myself that there's something new to be discovered, something new to be learned every day."

Vision

A vision is an overall idea of what an organization should do. It often reflects the dream of the founder or leader, as well as the core values and the purpose of the organization. A company's vision is its North Star. It is immutable, omnipotent, and omnipresent. It never changes. It guides everything the company does.

Here are some examples of corporate vision statements—some quite simple, others more high-minded and ambitious.

- Apple: To bring the best user experience to its customers through innovative hardware, software, and services.
- Target: To help all families discover the joys of everyday life.
- Google: To organize the world's information and make it universally accessible and useful.
- J. P. Morgan: To be the best financial-services company in the world.
- General Motors: To earn customers for life by building brands that inspire passion and loyalty, not only through breakthrough technologies, but also by serving and improving the communities in which we live and work around the world.

Let's look at Apple's vision statement and its focus on user experience.

The company's vision is to make products and services useful and appealing to the customer. A technology may be cool, but if it doesn't help the customer, Apple won't market it. As Steve Jobs told Apple's World Developer Conference in 1997:

> The hardest thing is how does that fit in a cohesive, larger vision that is going to allow you to sell $8 billion, $10 billion of products a year. One of the things I have always found is that you [have] to start with the customer experience and work backward to the technology. You can't start with the technology and then decide where you are going to sell it.
>
> The vision we have tried to come up with for Apple is what incredible benefits we can give to the customer. Where can we take the customer? Not starting with let's sit down with the engineers and figure what awesome technology we have, and then figure out how we are going to market that.[4]

What made Jobs such an effective leader is that he never wavered from this vision, even in the face of withering criticism.

Strategy

A strategy is a plan or roadmap that shows how a company can achieve its vision. This may involve opening stores in certain geographic areas or targeting a specific customer demographic. A company's strategy explains how it plans to use its competitive advantages—whether that be a unique product or service, pricing power, or distribution reach—to achieve its vision.

Target's strategy relies heavily on offering seemingly high-end lifestyle merchandise at discount prices. To do this, Target partners with designers like Missoni, Kate Spade, Jason Wu, and Michael Graves to create exclusive collections of apparel, accessories, and home goods. They use these products to draw people to stores, where they are likely to purchase everyday items like food, office supplies, and toys as well. Target always wants you to buy more than you intended to buy, and they use their exclusive merchandise as their main bait.

Tactics

Tactics are specific actions, sequences of actions, and schedules a company engages in to carry out its strategy. General Motors' tactics over the years include negotiating contacts with the United Auto Workers Union to cut operating costs and boost efficiencies, offering promotions and discounts to consumers on certain vehicles, and lobbying the federal government for tax credits on electric vehicles.

LEE'S VISION

If Bruce Lee had specifically written a vision statement for his businesses, it would probably look something like this: To integrate the East and West by promoting Chinese culture and ideas to the world through the teaching and practice of kung fu.

When Lee first arrived in the United States, he quickly realized that the country had little knowledge of kung fu. "Bruce had a pretty clear idea of the kind of future he wanted," his wife Linda Emery Lee wrote. "[And he knew] how he was going to achieve it and how to reconcile his ambitions and dreams and whatever success came his way with the underlying principles of kung fu."[5]

Lee felt that kung fu was not only superior to other martial art forms, but that styles like karate and judo actually originated from it. Given his extensive training in wing chun under Ip Man, Lee believed he was the man to educate Americans about the ancient art. In a letter to Pearl Tso, he wrote:

> Kung fu is the best of all martial art; yet the Chinese derivatives of judo and karate, which are only basics of kung fu, are flourishing all over the US This so happens because no one has heard of this supreme art; also there are no competent instructors . . . I believe my long years of practice back up my title to become the first instructor of this movement.[6]

Moreover, for Lee, kung fu was not just about fighting, but rather a means to live a quality, meaningful life. It was both a martial art and a philosophy.

> One part of my life is kung fu. This art influences [me] greatly in the formation of my character and ideas. I practice kung fu as a physical culture, a form of mental training, a method of self-defense, and a way of life.
>
> My reason in doing this is not the sole objective of making money. The motives are many and among them are: I like to let the world know about the greatness of this Chinese art; I enjoy teaching and helping people; I like to have a well-to-do home for my family; I like to originate something; and the last but yet one of the most important is because kung fu is part of myself.[7]

But Lee, a product of both the United States and Hong Kong, eventually saw his mission, not just as spreading kung fu, but also as promoting the beauty of Chinese culture and art to Western audiences. His goal was to bring two civilizations together and encourage Westerners to see Asian men as more than weak, sexless, and passive creatures. In her book *The Life and Tragic Death of Bruce Lee*, Cadwell wrote:

> He was the first oriental superstar to bridge the chasm between the East and West, to contradict the outrageous stereotypes represented on film and TV . . . and had therefore become a hero to millions in Southeast Asia who identified with him and saw him as their champion.
>
> A lethal whirlwind of flying fists and blurring legs, his magic kick had taken Western audiences by storm as he spectactularly revealed mysteries known only to the Chinese for centuries. Single-handedly, he had made the whole world conscious of kung fu.[8]

Even more remarkable, Bruce Lee foresaw the possibilities of opening mainland China to the global economy years before the country did so.

China and the United States had been allies during World War II. But after the war ended, China fell into civil war, with Mao Zedong's communist forces eventually triumphing over the nationalist government in 1949. Over the next twenty-five years, the United States refused to recognize the communist government of China and the two countries even fought each other during the Korean War.

President Richard Nixon eventually started to make overtures to the Chinese. In November 1971, during Bruce Lee's only English-language television interview, Canadian host Pierre Berton asked him what he thought of Nixon's plans. Specifically, Berton wondered if improved relations between the United States and China would help American audiences accept him as a leading star. Lee responded:

I do think things of Chinese will be interesting for the next few years . . . Once the opening of China happens, it will bring more understanding.

More things that are different, you know? And maybe in the contrast of comparison, some new thing might grow. It's a very rich period to be in.

If I were born forty years ago and if I thought in my mind and said: "Boy, I'm going to star in a television series in America," well, that might be a vague dream. But right now, I think it might be, man.[9]

Lee never got to star in that hypothetical American television series, but his foresight about the potential opportunities that would arise from China/US economic ties proved remarkably accurate.

In February 1972, two months after the Berton interview, Nixon visited China, paving the way for the United States and China to establish full diplomatic relations at the end of the decade. Over the ensuing years, China opened its economy to the West and embarked on a widespread "soft power" campaign to promote Chinese culture and ideas. Since 2004, China has established dozens of programs at American universities and colleges to teach the Chinese language and burnish the country's reputation.

Today, China is the world's second largest economy, with an annual gross domestic product of nearly $15 trillion, second only to the United States. Consulting powerhouse McKinsey & Co. comments on this rise:

The increasing exposure of the rest of the world to China reflects China's increasing importance as a market, supplier, and provider of capital. China accounts for 35 percent of global manufacturing output. Although it accounts for only 10 percent of global household consumption, it was the source of 31 percent of global household consumption growth from 2010 to 2017, according to World Bank data. Moreover, in many categories including automobiles, spirits, luxury goods, and mobile phones, China is the largest market in the world, accounting for about 30 percent (or more) of global consumption. As we have noted, it was the world's second-largest source and second-largest recipient of [foreign investment] between 2015 and 2017.[10]

An aspect of this growth that would have been especially relevant to Lee is that China has overtaken North America as the world's largest box office.[11]

"It comes to the point where even on some of the biggest films that make tons of money around the world, like a *Fast and Furious* film or a Marvel superheroes movie, getting into China and making money there . . . can mean the difference between profit and loss,"[12] said Erich Schwartzel, author of *Red Carpet: Hollywood, China and the Global Battle for Cultural Supremacy.*

---

*"I will live the way I please
and achieve inner harmony
and happiness."*

LEE'S STRATEGY

Lee had two main strategies for carrying out his vision: opening schools and making movies. In his letter to Pearl Tso, Lee was quite specific about his plans to establish kung fu schools across the United States.

> There are yet long years ahead of me to polish my techniques and character. My aim, therefore, is to establish a first Kung Fu Institute that will later spread out all over the US. (I have set a time limit of ten to fifteen years to complete the whole project.)[13]

Lee opened his first school in Seattle, where Doug Palmer, then a sixteen-year-old high school student, signed up.

Palmer recalls first seeing Lee demonstrate kung fu at a street fair in Chinatown:

> He demonstrated the Sticky Hand, which is a way of kind of sparring with somebody; once you touch their hands, you continue wrist contact the whole time. And watching him do that with his students and none of them were able to beat him even when he closed his eyes was something I'd never seen before either.

I decided I wanted to meet the guy and maybe take lessons from him. So I kind of let the word out and asked a few Chinese-American friends about him.

Palmer found Lee's school challenging, but ultimately rewarding.

At the time, Bruce was teaching his variation of wing chun. And there was a lot of emphasis on exercises that would strengthen the ligaments and the joints so you wouldn't hurt yourself and tear something with the snapping punches and the snapping kicks. I realized that I wasn't as flexible as I thought.

He focused on some of the basic techniques: the straight punch, straight front kick, side kick, and then different techniques to block. With the slapping hand, you use one hand simultaneously to slap the opponents guard away and at the same time you execute a straight punch. Or the pulling hand where you would grab his wrist and pull his arm so he's extended out and with the other hand strike with the fist.

Bruce was always polite. You could see he had a temper, but he kept it under control. He was very open in terms of welcoming anybody to the class. Whatever race or background, if they were interested in learning. And he was also generous with his time. He was four years older than me and he seemed like kind of an older brother in a way that he was friendly, outgoing, had a sense of humor. But he was also the teacher.

Linda Lee Cadwell agrees that Lee had a natural talent for promoting his projects. When marketing his martial arts schools, he often cited statistics for crimes like mugging, assaults, and rapes as reasons for prospective students to learn self-defense tactics. Cadwell said:

One can easily see with what thoroughness and business acumen Bruce had set about the job of making his *kwoon* a success. As one who had studied psychology, he had an instinctive aware-ness of what would attract customers.[14]

But Lee eventually realized that opening schools could only get him so far. For one thing, he was a bit of a perfectionist who wanted to teach classes personally rather than hire other instructors to run them.

Lee also liked to teach people based on their needs, their condition, and their skill. He even de-signed unique workout regimens for each student. But there was only one Bruce Lee, and he couldn't be everywhere at the same time. Such intense focus on quality and personalization meant that Lee could not scale his business. Moreover, his schools did not generate a lot of income, and he had a wife and two children to support.

Bruce ultimately decided to shift his strategy. First, he needed financial security. Second, he needed to reach a lot more people more quickly if he wanted to fulfill his vision of spreading the vir-tues of kung fu.

The answer was Hollywood.

Lee had played several roles as a child actor in Hong Kong, but the prospect of a film career didn't seem realistic when he moved to the United States. For one thing, the few roles Hollywood offered to Asians at the time weren't exactly appealing. But his breakout role as Kato in *The Green Hornet* demonstrated the possibilities of how television and film could allow him to realize his vision. Although the series lasted only one season, it allowed Lee to introduce kung fu to millions of Americans. No one had ever witnessed such speed, energy, and agility before. And, unbenownst to him at the time, Kato's fame had also spread to Hong Kong, which allowed him to (re)launch his film career there in the early 1970s.

From *The Big Boss* to *Enter the Dragon*, the latter a co-production with Warner Bros., Lee's movies electrified audiences of all races in both Asia and the US—especially young Asian-Americans who lacked role models and African-Americans who admired how Lee used his fighting skills to combat oppression.

In 1969, in his now-famous note "My Definite Chief Aim," Lee clearly laid out his goals:

I, Bruce Lee, will be the first highest paid Oriental super star in the United States. In return I will give the most exciting performances and render the best of quality in the capacity of an actor. Starting 1970, I will achieve world fame and from then onward till the end of 1980, I will have in my possession $10,000,000.[15]

We'll talk more about this commitment in chapter 4.

LEE'S TACTICS

Bruce Lee was a master tactician. Faced with the institutional racism that dominated Hollywood at the time, he had to adapt and evolve constantly in order to implement his strategy and realize his vision.

For example, beginning with his experience on *The Green Hornet*, Bruce knew he had to seize control over his career if he wanted to succeed. Although he was a gifted martial artist, producers refused to give him big parts or many speaking lines because of his race and accent. So he started to write his own scripts and tapped into his network of Hollywood friends, including actors Steve McQueen and James Colburn, director Roman Polanski, and screenwriter Stirling Silliphant.

Lee's biggest tactical shift was to move to Hong Kong and start Concord Production, his own production company. He hoped to make successful movies that would make it impossible for Hollywood to ignore him, a tactic that led to Concord's partnership with Warner Bros. on *Enter the Dragon*.

Authors Steven Kerridge and Daren Chua explain:

[Concord gave Lee] the resources to focus on not only acting but the added challenge of directing and producing his next movie. His belief in raising the bar, as far as Hong Kong movies were concerned, was a balance between art and commerce, which apart from providing a financially fruitful business model, would allow artistic control on all aspects of his future work.[16]

Despite a sizable temper, Lee was an expert tactician. He knew how to work people—when to employ flattery and when to apply hardball pressure. He was also an expert marketer and often used the media to further his aims.

IN THE WORDS OF KEN HAO

Ken Hao is the Chairman and Managing Partner of Silver Lake Partners, a global technology investment firm with more than $88 billion in combined assets under management and committed capital, and a team of professionals based in North America, Europe, and Asia.

Over the past twenty-five years, Hao has led investments in a wide range of technology industry leaders both in the United States and in Asia. Silver Lake is also a large investor in Endeavor Group Holdings, a global sports and entertainment firm that owns the Ultimate Fighting Championship (UFC), the premiere league for mixed martial arts (MMA) fighting.

Hao's recollections of the impact Bruce Lee had on his life are revealing.

As a child, I remember my parents talking about Bruce Lee a lot. I loved kung fu movies but I never really saw him in a movie until we went to see *Enter The Dragon*. And it was just electric, particularly the opening sequence, which I still think is the greatest of all time. It was a mind-blowing, riveting moment.

I'm sure it's a cliché by now, but a Chinese-American kid like myself needed a galvanizing, motivational hero. When I was growing up, Bruce Lee enabled this notion that all Asian-American guys knew martial arts. Obviously, that wasn't true in my case, but I enjoyed the compellingly cool element of this persona in contrast to the various negative stereotypes of Asian-American males.

When I was living in Hong Kong fifteen years ago, I reconnected with the Bruce Lee myth when I saw a *Wall Street Journal* ad from an auction house marketing a yellow pair of shoes from *Game of Death*. It brought back a flood of memories and restimulated my passion for Bruce Lee but with the added perspective of a mature adult.

The extraordinary amount of information on the Internet further enhanced my curiosity. I went back and found the photos and picture books about Bruce Lee that I collected in my youth. I started learning more about his personal philosophy rather than just his action photos. I'm just a sucker for inspirational quotes and he generated a treasure trove of them. His quotes are just unbelievable—the way he would phrase things and how insightful and deep they were. People can apply them to their personal lives.

I love the one where he says: "I fear not the man who's practiced a thousand kicks. I fear the man who's practiced one kick a thousand times." It just goes to show the discipline that he treasures. There's another quote in which he described how he valued love: "Love is a red hot coal that burns for a long time versus a flame that will just be bright and burn out quickly." I like that a lot too. I've been married for twenty-five years and I think about love and marriage as an enduring thing.

I admired the breadth and depth of his intellect, how he kept pushing himself to the highest levels of performance, how much he read and absorbed, and how he blended his personal philosophy into everything he did. And then I studied a lot of his writings. I actually ended up collecting a lot of his books from his personal collection that contained his handwritten notes. Who knows whether he read every page of some very complex philosophy books but he'd write in the margins and it was just a neat thing to understand which passages he cared about.

I love reading his books about fighting methods. He internalized all of these amazing skills from different martial arts. And then he incorporated them into a very flexible format. He wasn't just about kung fu, which obviously was foundational. But he was much more focused on a synthesis of different styles. There's a depth and richness to his persona. He was a man so ahead of his time.

Many leading figures of the sports world draw inspiration from Bruce Lee too. His appeal to the African-American community is amazing, especially basketball players like Steph Curry or Kobe Bryant. So many players have their Bruce Lee edition shoes. I mean, what's more important to basketball players than their shoes, right? That's just the ultimate apex of reverence. They love his charisma and obviously his amazing quickness and performance. Bruce had it all in one package, which is just as mind-blowing to me.

My firm Silver Lake is an investor in a large media and entertainment company called Endeavor, which acquired the Ultimate Fighting Championship (UFC). When you look back to the opening sequence of *Enter the Dragon*, Bruce is fighting an opponent with a unique style of gloves that they now use in the UFC. He was also using different martial arts styles, including striking and grappling.

People call him the Father of the UFC and I believe he was. He inspired so many UFC fighters. I actually gave a couple of friends who are actually training in MMA [mixed martial arts] Bruce Lee's fighting-method book and they are fascinated by how he made a science out of it. The UFC, in my view, is one of the best manifestations of his art. He would have loved MMA—Brazilian jujitsu over here, wrestling over there, boxing over here. UFC is the ultimate current incarnation of Bruce.

The other thing Bruce was able to do was toggle between Hong Kong and the United States in an interesting way where he monetized his fandom in Hong Kong and leveraged that into America. There was a business strategy associated with that. So pretty savvy maneuvering, I think, between the specific and the scalable.

But I don't try to tie Bruce Lee too tightly into how to run a business or be an entrepreneur. It's more about personal development and performance. How to be a high-performing individual.

The easiest analogy would be like a professional athlete preparing for the Olympics, practicing over and over and over again, and facing fears, understanding how to recover from failure. In the business world, consistently achieving the highest performance is what we all strive to do in our own way.

CHAPTER 3

Innovation, Bruce Lee Style

Humans are hardwired to spot patterns. Scientists have actually identified the region of the brain responsible for this—the neocortex, the outer layer of the brain, which accounts for 80 percent of the organ's weight.

Spotting patterns can be a good thing. Early humans were more likely to survive in a dangerous world when they could recognize that a particular plant was poisonous or that predators frequented the same watering hole during a certain time of day. Today, engineers create increasingly powerful software to identify relationships in vast amounts of data and train artificial intelligence to reason more like humans.

But the need to see patterns can also lead to lazy, faulty group-thinking, particularly for businesses. If we can turn data into a pattern or rule, then, according to neuroscientist and author Daniel Bor, "near-magical results ensue. We no longer need to remember a mountain of data; we need to only recall one simple law."[1]

This is especially true for startups in Silicon Valley, which like to think of themselves as original, disruptive innovators. But the reality is that these companies tend to copy other successful startups, because they see patterns in the data and conclude that what worked for those firms will work for them as well. Instead of following their own path, the firms act on what they assume is a set of rules based on previous patterns in hopes of success.

For example, Internet startups for much of this century tended to adopt open-floor seating plans and decorations like red British telephone booths because, ironically, they thought such an environment would stimulate creativity.[2] Worse yet, startups raised enormous sums of venture capital regardless of whether they actually needed the cash because . . . well, that's what successful startups *do*.

Scott Sonenshein, professor of management at Rice University, points out that companies started to think that success was dependent on their intake of resources:

> When you are surrounded by all of these signals that measure success, you start to play these games. You are not a real business unless you have a big office. That building isn't good enough because [you] look at the guy down the street and his building is bigger.[3]

Reliance on patterns can also hurt established corporations with a long track record of success. "A lot of companies are stuck in their traditional business models and don't move forward," notes Lee Huang, former executive at Barnes & Noble who helped launch the e-reader Nook. "They're not able to look a step or two ahead at where the customer or the market is really going."

Take Target Corporation. For most of its history, the retailer had thrived thanks to its "cheap chic" approach to merchandising and marketing, selling seemingly upscale apparel and accessories at affordable prices. They created what they believed was an immutable playbook to run the company, no matter the time or circumstance. Target's top management team, including the CEO, always came from people who rose through the ranks of the company and thus were well-versed in the "Target Way." The company did not hire outsiders to fill key executive roles.

But Target's success, like that of many retailers, was based on a business model in which people only frequented physical stores. As more consumers switched to online shopping, Target found itself outmatched by Amazon and other Internet competitors. They tried to build out their digital business but continued to struggle.

In 2011, the company debuted its most ambitious merchandising effort yet—a partnership with Italian fashion house Missoni to create a limited collection of clothing and accessories. But the company's website crashed. Some consumers couldn't access the site; others didn't receive orders even after Target had charged their credit cards.

As it turned out, Target failed to test its website properly in the months leading up to the Missoni rollout. The person who oversaw the website was not on the senior leadership team but was rather a mid-level manager. It was one of the most embarassing moments in Target's history. The company desperately needed a fresh perspective, someone not wedded to the retailer's outdated playbook and past successes.

Finally, in 2014, the company hired Brian Cornell as CEO, the first outsider in Target's history to lead the company. Since then, Target has reclaimed its dominance because Cornell could successfuly integrate online and physical-store operations.

Target's experience is a perfect example of how patterns, especially ones that have produced historical success for some firms, can tempt companies to lean on repetitive historical behaviors instead of forging a unique path suited for the present and future.

A NEW DIRECTION

Lee refused to fall into this trap. He realized that, to implement his vision, he needed to take a different path. So he developed a strategy of innovation that he applied, not only to his films, but to all his endeavors. The strategy was based on six tactics: break the rhythm, keep it simple; make it unique; make it real; focus on character; and educate audiences. Let's take a look at how he implemented each of these tactics.

Break the Rhythm

Bruce Lee hated patterns. He believed static systems stifled human potential, because they discouraged adaptation, creativity, and critical self-examination. Worse yet, blind adherence to patterns and tradition reinforced humanity's worst impulses, including racism, bigotry, and violence.

Lee firmly believed that people should constantly challenge previously held beliefs and assumptions:

> By an error repeated throughout the ages, truth, becoming a law or a faith, places obstacles in the way of knowledge. Method, which is in its very substance ignorance, encloses truth within a vicious circle. We should break such a circle, not

by seeking knowledge, but by discovering the cause of ignorance.[4]

People should not fear to be wrong. Otherwise, how can people improve themselves if they cling to outdated ideas and flawed "truth"?

In fact, tradition is nothing, but a formula laid down by experience. As we progress and time changes, it is necessary to reform this formula.[5]

"Set patterns, incapable of
adaptability, of pliability,
only offer a better cage. Truth is
outside of all patterns."

In combat, Lee said, two opponents engage in a sort of a dance in which they mirror each other. The key, he argued, is to find the "broken rhythm," a moment when you can disrupt an opponent's pattern of movement by striking when and where it is least expected.

Ordinarily, two people (of more or less equal ability) can follow each other's movements. They work in rhythm with each other. If the rhythm has been well established, the tendency is to continue in the sequence of the movement. In other words, we are "motorset" to continue a sequence. The person who can break this rhythm can now score an attack with only moderate exertion.[6]

This technique can also apply to life in general, Shannon Lee observed:

In combat, Bruce's form of disruption is to create an opening to strike. In life, we have our own habits and patterns, and if we can disrupt that rhythm then progress can be made and new things can be allowed into our life.

In the combat analogy, Bruce says you can break the rhythm through a small hesitation or a large unexpected shift or change. This way of disruption can be applied to life as a way to shift ourselves off of our plateaus and go to the next level. We all get stuck in patterns or loops in life.

If we are in our practice of wanting to level-up and grow, can we look at our lives to see where we are stuck in a pattern? How can we disrupt that pattern? How can we break that rhythm to move forward?[7]

To effectively innovate, Lee believed, a person needs to disrupt patterns and find an opening in the status quo in which to "break the rhythm."

Innovations can be groundbreaking, like editing DNA to prevent genetic diseases and converting sunlight into electricity. But most innovations are incremental; they consist of improvements to things that already exist. Innovation, or at least the idea for one, need not be difficult, just useful or compelling. Paul Graham, a venture capitalist and entrepreneur who founded Y Combinator in San Francisco argues:

People believe that coming up with ideas . . . is very hard—that it *must* be very hard—and so they don't try to do it. They assume ideas are like miracles: they either pop into your head or they don't.

When someone's working on a problem that seems too big, I always ask: "Is there some way to bite off some subset of the problem, then gradually expand from there?"[8]

Keep It Simple

Steve Jobs was not a scientist. He was not an engineer. He was not a mathemetician. He didn't invent the personal computer, the MP3 player, the tablet, or the mobile phone. His innovation was to make each device simpler and easier to use, often by eliminating technical features, sometimes by adding new ones.

When Jobs introduced the first iPhone in 2007, he argued that simplifying smartphones was in itself revolutionary:

The most advanced phones are called smartphones. They typically combine a phone, e-mail, and a baby Internet. The problem is that they are not smart and they are not so easy to use. Regular cell phones are not so smart and they're not so easy to use. Smartphones are definitely a little smarter, but they're harder to use. They're really complicated. Just for the basic stuff, people have a hard time figuring out how to use them. What we did is make a leapfrog product that is way smarter than the mobile device has ever been and supereasy to use.[9]

Simplicity, of course, doesn't mean simple-minded. In fact, it takes a lot of work and innovation to take complicated ideas and technology and strip them down to something that's elegant, efficient, and essential.

Bruce Lee also believed deeply in simplicity. He initially trained in wing chun, a form of kung fu, and then familiarlized himself with all forms of martial arts, including karate, tae kwan do, and judo. But he eventually concluded that all of these martial arts were overcomplicated and showy— long on presentation and aesthetics, but short on efficiency and effectiveness. The goal of martial arts, he believed, was to inflict maximum damage on an opponent with the least amount of energy.

Ruben Dua, founder and CEO of the video app Dubb and a martial artist himself, observed that Lee stressed simpilicity as a means to meet goals without wasting precious time and energy. In combat, he said, a person wants each strike to be "faster, quicker, and more forceful" than the opponent.

The same applies to business, Dua claimed:

> New companies can't match the resources of larger competition so they must keep things simple, get to the core of something through the efficiences of action. To generate the best results, use the longest weapon against the closest target. This means using the most effective medium to connect with the most ideal client.

Dua built his video sales system on the premise that if Dubb sends prospects a video message, they are much likelier to connect, trust, and do business with the company.

Lee also applied these concepts to his acting. In 1966, he wrote a letter to William Dozier, producer of *The Green Hornet* television series, asking for more speaking lines for his character Kato. Dialogue, in addition to the action sequences, could more fully flush out the character to its simplest—and most authentic—form, Lee argued.

> Simplicity—to express the utmost in the minimum of lines and energy—is the goal of kung fu, and acting is not too much different. I've learned to be "simply human" without unnecessary striving. I believe in Kato and am truthfully justifying the physical action economically.[10]

Make It Unique

Bruce Lee and Steve Jobs also shared another crucial trait as innovators. They both took existing things and combined them in ways that created something unique. Apple didn't just sell individual computers, smartphones, and tablets. Instead, the company sold an integrated *ecosystem* of products and services in which consumers could seamlessly purchase, access, and share their data and content across the various devices, whether a Macbook or an iPod. The system encouraged consumers to stay loyal to the Apple brand because they were so invested in this ecosystem.

Bruce Lee's greatest innovation was integrating the two sides of his identity—East and West—into an art that appealed to both cultures. Specifically, he fused the kinetic, dynamic action of Hong Kong kung fu movies with the characters and story-driven nature of Hollywood films in ways that elevated mass entertainment to a new level of ambition and excellence.

"Absorb what is useful, discard what is useless, and add what specifically is your own."

"Bruce Lee wasn't afraid to put himself out there," Dua said. "He used Hollywood as a vehicle to reach new audiences, to evangelize something he thought people should know about." As a result, his movies became global blockbusters that disrupted the industry by appealing to a broad range of audiences.

Bruce Lee didn't invent kung fu cinema. But like Steve Jobs and the computer, he took it to new audiences and created new possibilities. The genre was born in Hong Kong as the city, then under British rule, developed into a bustling international hub for commerce and light manufacturing in the 1950s. Kung fu cinema, which combined the passion of traditional Chinese opera with the acrobatic choreography of ballet, provided audiences a welcome escape from the stress of living in an overcrowded city. These films reflected what it meant to be Chinese. "Filmmaking wasn't just entertainment, but also a way of postulating the Chinese identity," Hing Chao, founder of the Hong Kong Culture Festival, explained.[11]

In the 1960s, the Shaw Brothers Studio, run by Run Run Shaw, dominated kung fu cinema, often producing and releasing several films in a single week. The poorly made but highly profitable movies helped the studio generate well over $2 billion each year in today's dollars. Films like *One-Armed Swordsman* and *The Chinese Boxer* tapped into the social unrest of the latter part of the decade by offering revenge tales that featured enormous amounts of violence. "I can guess what the people want better than most of the other producers," Shaw once bragged.[12]

Shaw Brothers resembled the old studio system of the Golden Age of Hollywood, in which companies like Warner Bros., MGM, and Universal controlled the production and distribution of movies. With such clout, the studios often signed movie stars to exclusive, multi-year contracts. Film historian Grady Hendrix claims:

> Shaw Brothers was the Death Star of Hong Kong movie studios. They would own their stars. They would own their own actors. They would own their own fan magazines. They would own their own sound stages, composers, and editors, cameras, and lights, and everything.[13]

But such domination made Shaw complacent, Hendrix argues.

> Shaw Brothers' problem in the 1970s was they were too big. They were too powerful. They had no reason to second guess their decisions. All of their decisions had been really right for a real long time.[14]

Shaw Brothers' greatest mistake? The studio failed to recognize Bruce Lee's potential.

Lee arrived in Hong Kong in 1971, hoping to reinvigorate an acting career that included some Hollywood successes, like the *The Green Hornet*, *Here Comes the Bride*, and *Longstreet* television series, and an appearance in the film *Marlowe*. Shaw didn't think much of actors. Still, Lee was already attracting considerable attention from audiences in Hong Kong because of the *The Green Hornet*. So Shaw made a low-ball offer to Lee: $2,000 a film and probably on a six-year contract, which was the standard Shaw deal.

Lee had good reason to ask for script details. He knew that Shaw's movies were poorly made, and that the studio pumped out films as if they were a factory.

But when committing to something, Lee always believed in doing things well. And by partnering with Raymond Chow and Golden Harvest Studios, Lee saw an opportunity to innovate within the Hong Kong film industry by infusing it with Hollywood professionalism and a strong focus on story and character development.[15] According to Cadwell:

> He realized that people wanted to see him as a fighter, but his characters had to have greater depth, to have individual personality. No other actor in Hong Kong had ever taken such a step. He was an innovator; a creator—a man who shaped rather than was shaped by events.[16]

Perry Yung, who stars as Father Jun in *Warrior*, describes Lee as a creature of both Hollywood and

Hong Kong cinema and claims it showed in his work:

> Bruce was a great storyteller. When you look at Hollywood storytelling, they're very character-based, on who is the lead, who are these characters, these actors? How do they tell the story? How do they take what's written and become a character that people can identify with?
>
> Bruce may have been influenced [by] his time in Hollywood, . . . seeing how . . . American actors approach[ed] a role, and applying that [knowledge] to the kung fu star. Prior to that, you see these amazing virtuosic martial arts skills, but the characters may be somewhat flat compared to what we think of as Hollywood actors.

Make It Real

Lee felt the martial arts had become too showy and impractical, so he sought to inject some believability into the over-the-top fight choreography that dominated kung fu cinema. Lee not only choreographed the action, he performed his own stunts to give the scenes a sense of heightened realism. Today, Hollywood stars like Tom Cruise, Jason Statham, and Keanu Reeves earn plaudits for performing their own stunts. But thanks to his natural athleticism and physical gifts, Lee pioneered the practice in the early 1970s, all without the benefit of special-effects technologies like CGI.[17]

Instead of actors and dancers, Lee recruited real martial artists to perform in his movies, including Bob Wall (*Enter the Dragon*), Kareem Abdul-Jabbar (*Game of Death*), and Chuck Norris (*Way of the Dragon*). "He believed (such casting) would give his film(s) added tension, authenticity, and genuiness," Cadwell tells us.[18] In Bruce Lee movies, the characters don't fight without end. They get hurt, even Lee himself. They have to adapt to their circumstances, and even fight dirty.

During Lee's famous fight scene with Chuck Norris in *Way of the Dragon*, the two combatants spend the first two minutes of the scene warming up, stretching limbs, cracking joints, and practicing kicks and punches.[19] When the fight begins, Norris, a karate expert, gets the best of Lee, knocking him to the ground several times. While lying on the ground, Lee rips off a chunk of Norris' chest hair. Bloodied, he realizes he must shift tactics.

Lee knows he won't win a brawl with a larger, stronger opponent. So he adopts the stance of a boxer. As his feet rhythmically bounce up and down, he circles Norris, changing the pace of the fight. He eventually overcomes Norris with a flurry of punches and well-placed kicks to vulnerable sections of Norris' legs, immobilizing him.

Focus on Character

Lee, however, wasn't just focused on the technical aspects of the fight. He wanted the fighting to say something about the characters themselves and the nature of violence. He wanted the fighting to advance the storyline. Kung fu films prior to Lee's arrival had been blood-soaked revenge fantasies that titilated audiences and left no doubt that the action trumped what little character depth and plot existed. But Lee saw the action *as* character and used that to make his films richer and more nuanced.

Lee felt that most martial arts movies were awful. The choreography was over-the-top and didn't reflect the circumstances of a real-life fight. As he told television host Pierre Berton:

> I hope whatever picture I'm in would either explain why the violence was done, whether right or wrong or what not. Unfortunately, pictures [in Hong Kong] are done mainly for the sake of violence, like guys fighting for thirty minutes straight, getting stabbed fifty times![20]

In fact, Lee's most disruptive move was to portray characters who wanted to *avoid* fighting. In *Enter the Dragon*, a bully wants to provoke a fight with Lee's character on a ship.

"What's your style?" the bully demands.

"My style?" Lee asks. "You can call it the Art of Fighting Without Fighting."

Lee then suggests they take a smaller boat to a nearby island, implying he will fight the man there. The bully gets into boat, but Lee pushes it out to sea, stranding him to the laughter of other passengers.

Lee used violence only when neccesary. *Enter the Dragon* centers on an effort by a secret agent recruited by British intelligence to infiltrate a martial arts tournament on a private island run by a drug lord. In the tournament, Lee encounters O'Hara, one of the drug lord's henchmen who had murdered Lee's sister. Rather than take revenge at the expense of the mission, Lee plays along and defeats O'Hara. But when O'Hara attacks him from behind with broken bottles, Lee defends himself and kills him. The camera focuses on Lee's face for several seconds, which betrays a cathartic mix of both regret and satisfaction.

In Lee's films, violence never came cheap or easy.

Educate Audiences

Lee considered himself not just a martial artist, but a martial artist philosopher. In his quest to teach audiences about Chinese culture, he wanted the fight scenes in his movies not only to entertain but also to convey important principles about Chinese concepts like Daoism, particularly to help people achieve tranquility. Dr. Wayne Wong, a researcher and instructor with the Hong Kong Polytechnic University, describes how he went about this:

> Through such liminal space, Lee positions himself between the vernacular and the scholarly as a way to negotiate his ambiguous identity, not only as a Chinese-American who was born in San Francisco yet raised in Hong Kong, but also as an avant-garde martial art actor-practitioner who bridges the chasm between the traditional and the modern, the local and the global, and the performative and the practical.
>
> He sought to make a more detailed connection between cinematic kung fu and his martial arts philosophy through extended dialogue, intricate choreography, and sophisticated cinematography.[21]

In an early scene from *Enter the Dragon*, Lee asks one of his students to kick him.

"What was that?" Lee scolds. "An exhibition? We need emotional content," pointing to his head.

The student tries again.

"I said emotional content, not anger," Lee responds. "Now try again. *With me*. Don't think. *Feel*. It's like a finger pointing a way to the moon. Don't concentrate on the finger or you will miss all of the heavenly glory."

The scene was not in the original script, but Lee insisted that producers add it to the film. His character was teaching his student to live in the moment, to establish an emotional connection with his opponent.

Lee criticized martial arts as being too showy, throwing unnecessary moves to either intimidate opponents or impress audiences. But this made the actors self-conscious and caused them to pay too much attention to themselves and how others perceived them rather than focusing on their opponents. Just as actors must learn to connect with and react to each other in the given moment to give a truly authentic performance, so too must martial artists bring an emotional dimension to their fighting to make the combat authentic.

In this sense, Lee epitomizes the phrase "art imitates life." His movies reflected what he believed and what he wanted to accomplish in his life, an approach that was radically different from the mindless action of previous kung fu films. Even as a movie star, Lee held true to his vision of connecting East and West.

BRUCE LEE'S DILEMMA

Bruce Lee certainly did not lack confidence and vision. But he was hardly a loose cannon. In his quest to reach larger audiences with his Hollywood productions, Lee also worried about alienating Chinese crowds.

For example, Chinese kung fu cinema didn't feature the martial arts tournaments that seemed to be popular in the United States. In the rough streets of Hong Kong, people didn't learn martial arts to win tournaments or ponder big philosophical questions. For them, fighting was literally about life and death.

You can see how Lee resolves this dilemma in *Enter the Dragon*. In the O'Hara scene, he kills his sister's murderer, but only in self-defense when O'Hara breaks the rules of the tournament. But the movie also features all-out brawls with Lee fighting off larger numbers of opponents in underground caves with nunchuks. He also added scenes like the one in which he explains to his student about his martial arts philosophies. There was something for everyone here. Clearly, Lee was a man who carefully thought about his audiences.

There is a lesson in this for businesses as well. Companies need to recognize how much innovation is too much. Take Best Buy, for instance, the world's largest consumer electronics retailer.

In 2006, the company opened its first big-box store in Shanghai, China. Four years later, Best Buy expanded to Europe. Both ventures failed because Best Buy assumed that the big-box format, a very American concept, would work overseas. But in Europe, especially England, people still preferred to shop for electronics at smaller local retailers. In China, consumers liked to go to malls or order online. Best Buy started to teeter toward bankruptcy as consumers flocked to online retailers like Amazon. Without foot traffic, the retailer was hard pressed to justify paying for leases for large stores that were essentially empty.

When Hubert Joly took over as CEO in 2012, analysts pressured him to close stores to cut costs. But Joly knew that closing stores would spell doom for Best Buy. The company's true identity was its physical stores. The moment it abandoned that identity, it was over.

So rather than see the stores as liabilities, Joly viewed them as Best Buy's greatest strategic asset. About 60 percent of America lived within ten miles of a Best Buy, something Amazon could never match. Joly saw that the problem wasn't that Best Buy operated stores, but rather how the retailer was using those stores. Under Joly, the company decided to reposition the stores as mini-warehouses, in which the company could fill online orders with merchandise from the physical site's inventory.

He also partnered with the company's top vendors like Microsoft, Samsung, and Sony to create "stores-within-stores" inside each Best Buy location. The concept boosted foot traffic and sales by providing each consumer with a unique experience when shopping for a particular brand.

Joly also realized that Best Buy wasn't even doing the little things well, like deploying a decent search engine on its website. Why blow up the whole house when you can just fix the sink and the radiator? Attacking this kind of "low-hanging fruit" worked wonders to improve Best Buy's overall numbers. Today, despite Amazon's dominance, Best Buy is one of America's top-performing retailers.

It may not seem obvious at first, but Bruce Lee and Joly held several things in common. Faced with challenging circumstances, they both knew the status quo wasn't acceptable. They also knew that they could not force themselves on foreign consumers without adapting to the local market.

At the same time, they recognized that they could still innovate while remaining true to their core identity. For Best Buy, that meant redefining the role of its physical stores to serve as a vehicle for e-commerce and to market top technology brands.

Bruce Lee knew everybody wanted him to kick ass. At the same time, Lee considered himself an artist and philosopher and wanted to convey deeper ideas to his audience through mass entertainment like kung fu cinema. After the success of *The Big Boss*, Lee said he wanted to make multidimensional films that offered audiences deeper meanings beyond the main plot.

So how successful was Lee in solving his dilemma, and did he innovate at the expense of his financial success? Hardly. His movies were huge blockbusters.

Lee's box office performance actually doesn't get the attention it deserves, especially when compared to Hollywood in general. In his quest to make higher-quality movies, he managed to secure more financing than the ultra-cheap kung fu flicks that Shaw Brothers produced. But the budgets behind Lee's films were still modest, especially by Hollywood's standards.

Nevertheless, Lee's films generated big numbers, both in terms of revenue and profitability.[22] Here's a profile of his films' profitability in the context of the film industry at the time:

- 1971—*The Big Boss*
  - Budget: $710,000
  - Box office: $355 million
  - Gross profit: $354.3 million
    - Top-grossing Hollywood film: *Billy Jack*
    - Budget: $5.6 million
    - Box office: $686 million
    - Gross profit: $680.4 million
- 1972—*Fist of Fury*
  - Budget: $688,000
  - Box office: $688 million
  - Gross profit: $687.3 million
- 1972—*Way of the Dragon*
  - Budget: $894,000
  - Box office: $894 million
  - Gross profit: $893.1 million
    - Top-grossing Hollywood film: *The Poseidon Adventure*

- ◆ Budget: $34 million
- ◆ Box office: $631 million
- ◆ Gross profit: $597 million

- 1973—*Enter the Dragon*
  - Budget: $5.5 million
  - Box office: $2.3 billion
  - Gross profit: $2.3 billion
    - ◆ Top-grossing Hollywood film:
      The Exorcist
    - ◆ Budget: $77 million
    - ◆ Box office: $1.2 billion
    - ◆ Gross profit: $1.2 billion

- 1979—*Game of Death*
  - Budget: $5.5 million
  - Box office: $1.1 billion
  - Gross profit: $1.1 billion
    - ◆ Top-grossing Hollywood film: *Grease*
    - ◆ Budget: $26 million
    - ◆ Box office: $590 million
    - ◆ Gross profit: $564 million

What's amazing about *Game of Death* is that the movie debuted five years after Bruce Lee's death. It wasn't even finished. But filmmakers managed to scrape together enough footage of Lee and combine it with footage of doubles to complete the film. As you can see, the movie was still a box office smash.

IN THE WORDS OF DUG SONG

Dug Song is the co-founder of Duo Security, the leading provider of two-factor authentication, a widely used technology that protects computer systems from unauthorized intrusions. In 2018, Cisco Systems purchased Duo for $2.8 billion. Song is now chief strategy officer for Cisco Secure.

Here's how Song describes the impact Bruce Lee had on him.

> I grew up watching Saturday morning kung fu shows on TV and remember seeing people that looked like me. It was actually pretty badass. Those shows really affirmed my own identity as an Asian-American. I already felt like a fish out of water, growing up where I did in the Washington, DC, area.

Maybe every boy who's a person of color in America had to kind of deal with that at some point. You learn about all kinds of heroes and warriors throughout US history. But growing up Asian-American, you don't really have anyone.

My dad looked like Bruce Lee and had the same haircut. But he didn't know martial arts and he was pretty mild-mannered. I worked at my dad's liquor store and he got mugged all the time. Once, he was stabbed eleven times. So people like Bruce Lee portrayed a vision of Asian masculinity that was absent from our experience.

A lot of martial arts is theory, more or less a kind of dance; it's a formalized ritual, a bunch of movements that are choreographed. It's great training, it's great exercise and coordination and so forth, but maybe not the most practical. I think in Bruce Lee's view, martial arts is actually about winning. There are things that work and things that don't. He is really driving toward what was true in practice versus in theory. You have to learn through trial and error. You could find your way to truth and what works.

When it came to actually starting a company, I did not want to follow someone else's footsteps. There's plenty to learn from the folks that have come before you, but there's nothing to say that you simply have to follow someone else's playbook. Why would we be any more successful copying someone else's playbook that they developed and trained on and perfected? There are things that we could take and borrow, things we could observe and try to incorporate. But at the end of the day, our truth will emerge just as it did for Bruce Lee, who adapted from the various forms, techniques, and practices that came before him.

In that sense, Bruce represented the American immigrant story. People do bring their histories from other countries with them, but they're not entirely bound by them. It gave me real comfort in being Asian-American. I could learn and appreciate the history from where my family originated, but I could forge my own path.

I knew children of immigrants who had a much harder time sort of finding their own way, because their parents constantly pressured them to fit into a sort of a model, a notion of what home culture was like from decades ago when they first left.

Bruce was someone who took the best of what worked for him into a new environment and made it uniquely his. He exemplified the American dream for lot of entrepreneurs.

In my early career, I used to spend a lot of time actually breaking into other people's security software. I quickly realized that the industry was like the emperor who had no clothes. It was a similar experience to Bruce Lee, like watching a whole history of martial arts that wasn't very effective. All these sort of styles and disciplines and they don't really work. This cybersecurity industry was full of products that were basically snake oil.

The vendor would sell you a box, kind of a piece of hardware you would put in your network. And nothing would happen. And the vendor would say: "See, you're more secure. Nothing's happening." And the customer thinks: "What did I just buy?"

And it took people like me, folks that had a bit of a chip on their shoulders, to poke and prod and ultimately break into those products, for people to realize that many of them weren't very good.

It was like Bruce's sparring matches, testing other people's martial arts disciplines, and realizing none of them worked. I was so disillusioned with that industry. It was something of a lemon market, where you buy a used car and you don't know if it's good or not until you drive off the lot, by which time it's too late. And again, a lot of computer security was like that.

I eventually left the industry to go do a TV company. But I came back when I saw a shift happening with the rise of the commercial Internet. More and more companies and organizations were getting online and not even just the big ones, like banks, hospitals, governments, but also your small retailers and corner coffee shops. All these folks were getting connected to the Internet and none of them had the skills with which to protect themselves or their technology.

And a lot of them were being targeted. By 2007, 2008, the American Banking Association had all this guidance around using a separate computer for online banking. An auto-body shop in Sterling Heights, Michigan, got popped. Someone wired $3 million out of their accounts. The bank at the time said: "Well, we're not liable. It's the customer's fault. They're the ones who got their password stolen." You sort of quickly realized that, wow, this is a really bad situation.

So my co-founder, Jon Oberheide, and I decided we would build a company to protect others from harm. Just as Bruce Lee wanted to share his knowledge, to share his gift, to share what he knew and understood about the world. With Duo Security, we had a mission to ultimately democratize security, of putting security within everyone's reach by making it easy and effective.

But it was not easy. The industry was hopelessly opaque and convoluted. It almost admired complexity, admired the problem versus actually solving it. In that early era of Internet security, there weren't as many people who had experience on both sides like myself and John, both as attackers and defenders. We knew what worked. And so we tried to simplify.

We also thought really deeply about empathy, for the plight of those users and how painful and onerous it was. We wanted to build better security, not just more security. We focused on highly integrated design, so design and product led to innovation. We wanted our technology to have personality; it didn't have to be cold or sterile or even scary for it to be effective.

At a time when the rest of the computer security industry was selling to the enterprise, to the 1 percent, we decided to go for the mass market. But that was hard because those people weren't looking for security, had never bought it before, didn't know sort of how to evaluate things. So we had to educate, we had to inform, in some cases we had to entertain.

There was plenty of security software out there that tried to terrify you with ominous red and black warnings and sensationalistic marketing. We tried to make everything approachable and accessible, to deliver things with some personality or some style so that it's intriguing and appealing. So our colors were green, meaning go, to offer a path right through all the chaos.

That's when I started to think about Bruce Lee's movies.

Those early kung fu films from Shaw Brothers were super flowy and campy. It took fifteen minutes of back and forth between two opponents for anything to really happen.

But Bruce Lee movies hit different. Literally. His punches and kicks were super fast. He would take on a room full of people coming at him. And you quickly realize that's what real combat looks like. You take someone out as fast as you can. He was like a flash of lightning. Whether ripping off his shirt or licking blood off his face, Bruce had style. He held your interest. The dude represented.

In the *Game of Death*, that yellow jumpsuit he wore? That was like the height of style, man. When you saw the jumpsuit, it was almost as if he was foretelling where things were going, that martial arts would become a mainstream thing.

A lot of that stuff is probably what attracted mass-market audiences to his films. Bruce was all about integrating pop culture into his movies. Casting celebrities and athletes like Kareem Abdul-Jabbar and Chuck Norris. It said something about what he did. It's contemporary, it's fresh, it's modern.

We tried do the same thing. We had a lot of swagger because we knew we could back it up. We used to talk about slogans: "Frustrate the attackers, not your users." We were pitting ourselves against the rest of industry, which was just junk. We would taunt the other products in the industry, how they were ineffective. It was almost like Bruce with his palm outstretched, wiggling his fingers at them, like: "Come on."

Our business really grew through word of mouth, which I think is the best way to grow business, and lots of customers referring to each other. There's a fine line between arrogance and confidence and that was something that Bruce embodied. You always rooted for that guy.

Bruce and Steve Jobs were big inspirations for what we did. Finding your own route to success is a process of trial and error, not blindly borrowing and stealing other things, but adapting and integrating them into something new.

It was about reducing things to their essentials. Perfection happens, not when there's nothing left to be added, but when there's nothing left to be taken away. That was the essence of Bruce and Steve Jobs. They streamlined things down to the core essential and in such a way that it itself represented a certain kind of aesthetic.

Bruce wasn't flat as a fighter. With every move, even when he was dancing around, it was to keep people off kilter. Those choices to omit or elevate something, they represent a strategy. People misunderstand that. All they see is that they just took away a lot of stuff. It's almost too simple.

People ask us all the time: "Wait, so you're just doing two-factor authentication? That's all you're building? That's just a feature." The technology was actually commercialized in 1985 and invented even earlier. And here I am in

2010, starting a company doing the same thing hundreds of companies had already done.

And I had already built some pretty sophisticated stuff, like artificial intelligence and machine learning systems for computer security, things that wouldn't hit until twenty years later. With two-factor authentication, my colleagues in the industry were thinking: "Wow, why are you doing something so simple, so easy?"

And I tell people: "Because it works." But the other piece was that we took a contemporary spin on it. We focused on mobile devices instead of hardware. In 2010, the iPhone was only two years old but was rapidly becoming popular. To me, applying two-factor authentication to smartphones and delivering it from the cloud was a little bit like Bruce Lee putting on a yellow-and-black jumpsuit.

No, you don't need do all these other things. You just need to do what works, what's efficient and effective. That summarizes a lot of Bruce's philosophy. The rest is just wasted motion or in many cases for our customers, wasted money.

You can buy all those lemon products that do nothing or you can do a couple things that will actually protect you. Steve Jobs is like that too. He took the best of what worked and stripped it down to its essentials. The resulting minimalism was an aesthetic in itself.

CHAPTER 4

Overcoming Adversity

In the United States, we admire the success of entrepreneurs—perhaps to a fault. We frequently forget that most entrepreneurs, like everybody else in life, failed more than they succeeded.

For example, Harland David Sanders, known popularly as Colonel Sanders, was sixty-nine years old, living off Social Security, and sleeping in the back of his car when he started to peddle his fried-chicken recipe to restaurants. By then, Sanders had already failed at law and several businesses, including a stint selling life insurance, before he was fired for insubordination. Amazon founder Jeff Bezos struck out with Pets.com, zShops, and LivingSocial.

And Apple famously fired co-founder Steve Jobs in 1985 after he clashed with CEO John Sculley.

But all of these people ultimately persevered and adapted. Jobs came back to Apple in 1997 a much better, less intractable leader, which Sculley himself admitted:

> The Steve Jobs that worked with me in 1985 never, ever would have created a product like iTunes and put it on Microsoft. When he came out with the iPod and iTunes, it was brilliant. It was exactly the right product. It reinvented the music industry, and he put it *on Windows.*[1]

Bruce Lee fits in this category as well—but with one important caveat: none of these other entrepreneurs, who are all caucasian, ever encountered setbacks because of the color of their skin.

Nonetheless, we can't examine Lee's successes without examining his failures. And we can't examine his failures without examining the deep-rooted institutional racism that permeated Hollywood at the time. Only then can we fully understand and appreciate Lee's unlikely emergence as a global movie superstar. As his friend Doug Palmer tells us:

> He was able to make his way against headwinds in Hollywood where Asian actors were not particularly esteemed. I think that struck a chord with a lot of people: his ability to prevail over all kinds of odds.

THE LEGACY OF YELLOWFACE

Chinese people first started to emigrate to the United States in the 1840s. Then, as well as today, companies wanted lower-cost labor and the Chinese answered the call. Over the next decades, they worked as miners, railroad laborers, and factory and restaurant workers, primarily in California, especially San Francisco, but in other parts of the West Coast as well.

The willingness of the Chinese to work for lower wages put them in the cross hairs of other immigrant groups and workers who feared they would lose power due to cheaper foreign labor. The resulting demonization of Chinese workers often led to violence and discrimination, and culiminated in the Chinese Exclusion Act of 1882, which banned Chinese immigration for ten years. The law was the first in American history to specifically target a single ethnic group.

The racism against Chinese was often reflected in and indeed enhanced by pop culture, specifically through what was known as "yellowface"— the casting of white actors in plays, television shows, and movies as Asian characters. The practice demonized Asians as inferior or as sinister foreigners who threatened America. Yellowface also portrayed Asian women in an overly sexualized, exotic manner. D. W. Griffith, best known for the highly racist *The Birth of a Nation*, which reignited interest in the Ku Klux Klan, actually released a short movie in 1910 called *The Chink at Golden Gulch.*

As movies gained popularity in America, Hollywood adopted the Hays Code, a set of informal rules that governed the industry from 1930 to 1968. One of these rules prohibited an actor of one race from having an on-screen romantic relationship with a person of another race. The rule effectively meant that non-whites could not gain leading roles, which gave producers the excuse they needed to cast white actors and actresses as Asian characters. Among these, we find Katherine Hepburn in *Dragon Seed* (1944), Warner Oland in the *Charlie Chan* films, John Wayne as Ghenghis Kahn in *The Conqueror* (1956), and Mickey Rooney in *Breakfast at Tiffany's* (1961). Suffice it to say, the only roles Asian-Americans could gain during this period were those of servants, sidekicks, and comic relief that reinforced historical stereotypes and racist caricatures.

This was the reality confronting Bruce Lee in the 1960s. And he was keenly aware of it.

Then a role came along that both changed everything—and changed nothing.

SEEN BUT NOT HEARD

Lee frequently taught and demonstrated his martial arts skills in communities along the West

Coast, and his work started to attract notice. In 1964, he attended a karate tournament in Long Beach, California, where he demonstrated several moves, including his famous one-inch punch and two-finger pushups. Hollywood television producer William Dozier caught wind of Lee's electric performances and cast the young martial artist in *The Green Hornet* as Kato, the sidekick to the show's eponymous hero.

Dozier was looking for a show that could exploit the popularity of the *Batman* television series. Just as Bruce Wayne was a billionaire playboy during the day, but a vigilante hero at night, *The Green Hornet* featured Britt Reid as a wealthy newspaper publisher who transformed into a masked hero at night.

But the series' real star was Reid's sidekick Kato, played by Lee, who introduced millions of Americans to kung fu. If Batman's gimmick was his gadgets and cars, the Green Hornet's was Lee's martial arts skills. His lightning-fast moves, which the cameras had trouble catching, electrified audiences, although critics were less receptive.

Kato proved to be a more popular character than the Green Hornet. His character received way more fan mail from kids, like Ricky McNeece of Clinton, Iowa, who asked for a Kato mask for a school project in the hopes his teacher would give him an A. Even negative reviews had some positive things to say about Kato's fighting ability. Those who watched him would bet on Lee to render Cassius Clay senseless if they were put in a room and told that anything goes.[2]

For Asian-Americans, however, Lee's role gave them their first opportunity to watch someone who looked like them playing the role of a strong and powerful character on a major television show.

The character's popularity was hardly enough for Lee, however. He wanted to grow and expand as an actor. And to do that, he needed speaking lines. Unfortunately, Dozier and the writers gave him precious few, even though Kato was by far the best thing about *The Green Hornet*.

For the *We Are Bruce Lee* exhibit in San Francisco, the Chinese Historical Society of America analyzed all twenty-six episodes of the series and found that, of the 6,099 seconds of screen time Lee performed as Kato, he spoke only 7 percent of the time. By contrast, Casey Case, the Green Hornet's secretary, had 3,476 seconds of screen time and spoke 22 percent of the time. The same imbalance was true of other characters in the show. Moreover, the imbalance did not apply to Batman's sidekick, Robin (see table on the following page).

To make matters worse, the show paid Lee far less than the other actors, who were all caucasian. Lee made $400 per week (the same as a stuntman) compared to $850 for Wende Wagner, who played Ms. Case, and $2,000 for Van Williams, the Green Hornet himself. When the series was canceled after only one season, Dozier wrote, in a condescending, racist-tinged letter to Lee: "Confucious say: Green Hornet buzz no more."

Unfortunately for Lee, the worst was yet to come. After *The Green Hornet* ended, Lee struggled to find work in Hollywood. He was offered bit parts, but nothing approaching the leading roles he believed he was destined to play. Roles like the

Green Hornet and Batman
Cast by Lines and Screen Time

CHARACTER	SPEAKING TIME	SCREEN TIME	%
Kato	438	6,099	7%
Ms. Case	774	3,476	22%
Britt Reid/ Green Hornet	5,138	14,692	35%
District Attorney Scanlon	1,176	2,966	40%
Mike Axford	1,161	2,504	46%
Robin	915	4,967	18%
Batman	1,951	6,121	32%
Gordon	513	1,180	43%
Alfred	202	749	27%

lead in the Warner Bros. series *Kung Fu* went to white actors like David Carradine, with Lee being offered the job as technical advisor. Although Lee worked extensively on a rewrite of the script and was considered by Warner Bros. executives for the lead, Hollywood's institutional racism torpedoed his hopes, despite the positive impression he had made on producer Thomas Kuhn:

> When he walked into my office . . . it wasn't hard to form a first impression of Bruce. He walked in, gym bag in hand, pulled out his nunchaku, and started to swing it at me . . . He put it away and then thrust his arm at me and said: "Feel my arm." And it was like steel. I mean, it was just unbelievable.[3]

Nonetheless, Lee received the following in a telegram from producer Jerry Leider:

> Dear Bruce, am terribly sorry to tell you that I was unable to work out the kung fu picture for you due to enormous differences of opinion and pressures from the network regarding casting of this picture.[4]

The "enormous differences" referred to producers saying they could not understand Lee's accent.

Judy Coppage, head of development for screenplay writer Stirling Silliphant, claimed:

> I believe the problem for Bruce was because of his accent. Asian actors back then were rarely cast for similar reasons, and this had certainly held Bruce back in Hollywood.[5]

But Lee spoke fluent English. Sylvester Stallone's slurred speech, the result of partial paralysis on the lower left side of his face, had not prevented him from making *Rocky* in 1976 and becoming a global superstar. Nor did a thick Austrian accent stop Arnold Schwarzenegger from achieving box office success in the 1980s and beyond.

What's more likely is that producers felt that American audiences would not accept a man of Asian descent as a leading man. To make matters worse, producers ultimately cast David Carradine, an actor with no martial arts experience, as the lead in *Kung Fu*, a role he reprised with the spin-off series *Kung Fu: The Legend Continues* in the 1980s.

Once again, the yellowface legacy had raised its ugly head. And it continues to do so. Tilda Swinton played a character who was originally Asian in Marvel's *Dr. Strange* (2016). Scarlett Johanssen was similarly cast to play the part of an Asian in *Ghost in the Shell* (2017).

That's not to say that things haven't improved for Asian-American actors, who have starred in commercial and critical hits like *Crazy Rich Asians* and *Shang-Chi and the Legend of the Ten Rings*. But Hollywood continues to remain overwhelmingly white. Online streaming giant Netflix commissioned a study from the USC Annenberg School of Communications and Journalism that examined the racial, ethnic, and gender make-up of the 126 original movies and 180 scripted series it released in 2018 and 2019. The study found that Asian actors accounted for only 2.3 percent of all leads and co-leads, even though the Asian community makes up nearly 6 percent of the US population. By contrast, white actors landed 72 percent of all leads and co-leads while accounting for only 60 percent of the population.[6]

Asians fared even worse behind the camera. They comprised 3.1 percent of all directors, 4 percent of writers, and 4.2 percent of producers. Whites accounted for 80 percent of all directors, 83 percent of all writers, 85 percent of all producers, and 88 percent of all creators. Not surprisingly, the study found that shows featured more actors who were people of color when directors, writers, and producers were also people of color.

Like Bruce Lee, Asian artists today often find they have to make the best of whatever work they can find, even though their artistic ambitions stretch far beyond what Hollywood is willing to offer.

BE WATER, MY FRIEND

The heart of Bruce Lee's philosophy is water, an ideal metaphor for people seeking calm and clarity in a cluttered, chaotic world. The liquid is clear and formless but ultimately takes on the shape of whatever it touches. Water is essential for life and represents the purest state of being, Lee believed.

And just as water can flow anywhere without limits, Lee believed that humans should pursue their potential without limits. Tradition and static systems like religion and martial arts schools merely stifled human potential because they discouraged adaptation, creativity, and critical self-examination.

"Be water, my friend," Lee advised:

> Empty your mind. Be formless, shapeless, like water. You put water into a cup, it becomes the cup. You put water into a bottle, it becomes the bottle. You put it into a teapot, it becomes the teapot. Now water can flow or it can crash. Be water, my friend.[7]

Bruce Lee was unique, in that he commanded a clear, integrated approach to his life. He was either incapable of or unwilling to compartmentalize events and ideas. There was no "leaving it at home" or "leaving it at the office" for him. Everything was connected—films, martial arts, family, philosophy, mind, body.

Physically, Lee was not an imposing figure. At his peak, he stood just over five and a half feet and weighed a scant 130 pounds. But his background as a champion ballroom dancer taught him agility and coordination. Speed and flexibility would always trump brute strength for him. And in order to perform his gravity-defying kicks and jumps, Lee placed great value on stretching and warming up, because he knew that his flexibility depended on his joints and the elasticity and firmness of his ligaments, as well as on the condition of his cartilage.

But Lee didn't just train his body to peak potential. He also fervently trained his mind. He believed that humans reach their fullest potential only when mind and body work together. To this end, he developed jeet kune do (JKD) as a philosophy for fighting. In reality, JKD was a philosophy for how to live life in general—not as a static system governed by rigid rules, but rather as a dynamic, ever-shifting experience in which you must absorb new information and adapt accordingly.

———————

"Notice that the stiffest tree
is most easily cracked, while
the bamboo or willow survives by
bending with the wind."

———————

In a real life fight, he knew that you must fully engage your opponent in the moment and then shift tactics and strategies depending on what the opponent shows you. Shannon Lee explains:

Most literally, the combative arts require one to be fully present and fluid to not get caught flat-footed and knocked off balance—or knocked out! You have to respond to the punch coming in order to avoid or block it. To be like water is to adapt in response to your environment and opponent. In other words, to be pliable.[8]

THE IMPORTANCE
OF FLEXIBILITY

In keeping with this philosophy, one major theme predominates in all areas of Lee's life—*flexibility*.

Lee used three specific stragies to maintain his flexibility, adapt to his situation, and overcome adversity: he worked within the system; he never hesitated to seize control; and he started fresh when necessary.

Work Within the System

Bruce Lee was no fool. He knew that Asians faced racism in Hollywood and that the country in general was accustomed to seeing white actors in lead roles. Pierre Berton asked him directly about this problem:

> Berton: Let me ask you, however, about the problems that you face as a Chinese hero in an American series. Have people come up in the industry and said: "Well, we do not know how the audience is going to take a non-American?"
>
> Lee: Well, such a question has been raised . . . that is probably why *Warrior* is not going to be on.
>
> Unfortunately, such a thing exists in the world. In a certain part of the country where

they think, business wise, it's a risk. And I don't blame them. It's like in Hong Kong, if a foreigner came and became a star, if I were the man with all of the money, I probably would have my own worry of whether or not the acceptance would be there.[9]

Lee was being highly diplomatic. But the truth is that racism stung and demoralized him.

Nonetheless, Lee kept trying because he believed in himself. He could have just quit the business. Or he could have openly complained about it—which, given the times, would have spelled the end of his career. But he just persevered, writing to Ted Ashley, a top executive at Warner Bros.:

I am sorry to hear about the outcome of *Warrior*. Well, you cannot win them all, but damn it, I am going to win one of these days.[10]

Some people see Bruce Lee as a civil-rights icon. But that would be misleading. He was not overtly political. He was certainly aware of the civil-rights struggles taking place in America in the 1960s. But there's no evidence to suggest that he actively participated in them. He did not give speeches, attend rallies, or march to Washington, D. C.

Instead, Lee believed in leading by example. And lead he did.

---

*"Whether I succeed or not
remains to be seen. But
I just don't feel committed.
I am committed."*[11]

Seize Control

At some point in his frustrations with *The Green Hornet*, Lee knew he had to act. Despite constantly lobbying Dozier for more speaking lines, Lee was largely silent in the series and the lines he did receive were mostly those of a servant.

Lee ultimately penned an episode called *Cobra from the East*, which gave him a much larger part. The producers never used it, but writing the script taught him a lesson that would shape the rest of his career. If Hollywood was never going to give him the roles he wanted, he would just have to create them himself.

After the *Green Hornet,* Lee wrote a script with screenwriter Stirling Silliphant and actor James Coburn called *The Silent Flute.* He also conceived the property that would eventually become *Warrior.* Although none of these projects were completed in Lee's lifetime, the experiences gave him an opportunity to stretch his creative muscles and develop the films that would best suit him.

In Hong Kong, Lee took a more active role in making *The Big Boss* and *Fist of Fury,* often to the annoyance of director Lo Wei. He not only starred in the films, but also choreographed the fight scenes and offered plenty of notes on the scripts. The box office success of both films gave him the confidence to start Concord Production with Raymond Chow. Cadwell describes it as a "time of decision":

He had to decide about his personal statement in regard to kung fu films. He was never satisfied to ride along on success; each film, he believed, would have to be better than its predecessor. And he felt the only way he could achieve this was if he had more control over all of the elements.[12]

Today, every A-list actor in Hollywood boasts a production company—Brad Pitt (Plan B Productions), Drew Barrymore (Flower Films), Tom Cruise (C/W Productions), Julia Roberts (Red Om Films). But it wasn't very common in the 1970s.[13] And certainly not for a minority actor.

Concord Production not only allowed Lee and Chow creative and financial control over their projects, it also gave them the neccessary mechanism to negotiate with Warner Bros. for *Enter the Dragon* on a more equal basis.

The birth of Concord would now give freedom to "honestly express himself" and prove his worth on an international stage, as he knew it wasn't the case that "if" Hollywood came knocking, but more so "when."[14]

Start Fresh

After ABC canceled the *The Green Hornet*, Lee's career floundered. He was broke and had a wife and two kids to support. So against the advice of some of his Hollywood friends, Lee relocated to Hong Kong to find work. As it turned out, it was the best move he could have made. He didn't know it at the time, but *The Green Hornet* had just debuted in Hong Kong and audiences there loved it. They even renamed it *The Kato Show*. Right off the bat, Lee found himself with a fan base.

> I didn't know what was going on. Green Hornet was a big hit with the people there and they kept replaying it for months. I guess I'm the only guy who ventured away from there and became an actor. To most people, including the actors and actresses, Hollywood is like a magic kingdom. It's beyond everyone's reach and when I made it, they thought I'd accomplished an incredible feat.[15]

But a star makes his own luck, and Lee fully intended to exploit his fame. He could easily just have sat back and enjoyed his newfound success in Hong Kong. But his vision was to integrate East and West, and to do that, he needed Hollywood, the same institutional system that had snubbed him over and over because of his race.

Cadwell said Lee's goal was to make hits in Hong Kong so that studios would have to notice him again.

> Bruce *wanted* Hollywood to approach him. With the reapproachment between China and the United States a new factor in world politics, he realized his chances of breaking into the international market, of becoming the first Chinese world superstar in history, were no longer an impossible dream. The bamboo and dollar curtains had been pierced and America, still the greatest world cinema power, was ripe to accept an Oriental hero.[16]

As *The Big Boss* and *Fist of Fury* generated enormous box office results, Lee made sure Warner Bros. knew about it, writing this to Ted Ashley:

> Presently, [Hong Kong] will be my base of operations as my films are enjoying "unbelievable"

success. If Warner develops something specific for me, I'm sure my special brand of action will sock it to them.[17]

Lee's tactics worked. If Warner Bros. had any doubt about Lee's ability to carry a movie, those doubts were gone by now. In a letter, Ashley responded:

Dear Bruce, I'm delighted that your second film is heading for another record. I couldn't be happier for you.

I want you to know that I appreciate the suggestion offered by Mr. [Raymond] Chow and yourself that you would give us the first opportunity of examining the projects which you finally wish to do on a co-production basis.[18]

By the early 1970s, Hollywood was looking for something new. The studio system was defunct and the industry was moving away from lavish, large-scale productions in favor of grittier, less expensive films. This is the era that produced "New Hollywood" directors like Francis Ford Coppola,

Martin Scorcese, Steven Spielberg, Brian DePalma, and George Lucas.

In 1972, Warner Bros. finally agreed to co-finance and distribute the film that would become *Enter the Dragon*. Ashley telexed Lee on January 15, 1973:

> I know that this week you start production on *Enter the Dragon*. I want you to know that, not only I, but all of my associates are genuinely very enthusiastic about the script and believe that the movie with you in it will fulfill all of the hopes which you and I discussed in my office many months ago.
>
> I also believe that the merit of the picture coupled with the effort which Warner Bros. will put behind it should result in a truly international motion picture which will serve as the foundation of a continuing relationship between us.[19]

The studio only put up a modest $800,000 for the film, but the deal marked the culmination of all Lee's hopes and dreams.

IN THE WORDS OF VIJOY RAO

Vijoy Rao is an entrepreneur in St. Louis and an adjunct professor of business at Maryville University. He is a former top executive at Fleishman Hillard, one of the nation's largest public relations firms.

Rao describes his keen awareness of the impact that Bruce Lee had on his life and his career.

I first saw Bruce Lee movies on Saturday morning television when I was like nine or ten. Like everyone else, I was just immediately captivated. I never had seen anything like him before or since. All of the action. All of the speed. "Wow, that spinning tornado kick's amazing! Wow, he jumped and kicked the light off the ceiling just by standing still!" That was amazing, you know? I just went down the rabbit hole in just becoming a lifelong fan.

What's great about Bruce Lee is that he was not just a phase that you go through: "Oh yeah, I used to like Bruce Lee, because I used to like kung fu movies." With Bruce Lee, as you grow up, you realize there's more and more. You just keep rediscovering Bruce Lee. Depending on where you are in life and what you're doing, you always end up going back.

He was incredibly intelligent and just spectacularly self-aware. He was incredibly entrepreneurial and he was incredibly creative. There are still things about him that you're discovering and rediscovering that are relevant to your life regardless of how old you are or what you're doing. His philosophies were all relevant to just growing up and being an adult. Don't wish for an easy life, but wish for the strength to endure a difficult one.

I tell myself that every single day. All this stuff is beyond just kicking and fighting and having great action scenes. There are just a lot of really cool and deep things that go beyond just maybe what you liked about him initially.

Instead of being perceived as being something, whether you're a business or a person, just be the thing. Remember that scene in *Enter the Dragon* when O'Hara tries to intimidate Bruce by breaking a board? Remember what Bruce said? "Boards don't hit back." Don't try to look as if you're the thing. Be the thing. Don't fall for that fake, meaningless ability that isn't really applicable in real life or in what you're really doing.

Every scene in his movies seems to have broader, more profound lessons. In *Way of the Dragon*, after Bruce defeats Chuck Norris, he's very respectful at the end. I think that's important for business as well. To respect competitors, you know? There's no one else that understands what it's like in the trenches better than your competitors. No one else can really understand what you're going through on a daily basis.

One of things that I learned from Bruce is that, as an entrepreneur, you have to be able to do a lot with a little. When you're building a business from scratch, every single buck has to act like a hundred dollars at least. You have to be able to do a lot with a little. Just like Bruce's one-inch punch.

I first got the idea for Magic Room Brand, an online music supply business, at the end of 2015 and officially launched it toward the end of 2016. The company designs and delivers eco-friendly musician accessories like picks and drumsticks.

I'm a drummer and guitar player. And one of the things about being a drummer and guitar player specifically is that the guitar picks and drumsticks you use wear down fast and are not good for the environment.

Guitar picks are generally made out of different kinds of petroleum-based plastics. Drumsticks are made out of wood. And you would think they'd be biodegradable but they're usually coated with a ton of chemicals to harden them. And they're not very sustainable or eco-friendly at all.

I've been a musician for over thirty years and kind of waited for someone to come up with an eco-friendly option. And then finally, I was just thought: "You know what? I'm going to give this a whirl." So I decided to step out and create this business on my own.

It's been quite a journey. Hands down the hardest thing I've ever done professionally.

I used to work at Fleishman Hillard, a public relations firm. And in marketing and communications, we want to tell clients do this and do that and then charge them. It's a different animal entirely when you're your own client, you know?

My late father was a doctor. When he was in the hospital, it was just sort of common knowledge that doctors make the worst patients because they've got the burden of knowledge. They know how things are supposed to be. And when they're in that room, they're used to being in a different role.

So all the things I used to do for other Fortune 100 companies, to do it yourself in making sure that, man, every buck has to be like at least a hundred dollars worth of effort here [is tough]. And out of the five things that need to be done today, I can maybe get to one of them. I have to understand, okay, what's the priority? What's most important?

I can't just yell out of my office to a world-class graphic designer and have them bang something out that looks amazing and totally professional.

I can't go three doors down and talk to an SEO expert or go talk to a video production expert that's two doors down. I have to do everything.

In *Fist of Fury*, Bruce Lee was surrounded by karate guys in a dojo. In business, in marriage, in real life, problems surround you. Problems aren't polite enough to get in line and come at you one at a time. They're not going to wait for their turn. They're going to surround you and constantly come at you from different angles.

In business, you have to prioritize. Prioritization is probably the #1 most important thing to do when you're starting a business. Being able to have a 360° view of what's coming at you, how severe the situation is. Can I vanquish them immediately or do I kick them back and then buy myself some time and handle some other things and come back to that guy later?

So to be an entrepreneur, you have to rewire your whole brain: "I don't know how to do this, but it has to be done and it's got to be me, so let's figure this out." Not really understanding how to do something, but then doing it anyway. And then falling down, getting back up, and then figuring out. And eventually you get a little bit more conversant and a little bit better at some of these things.

That's the hard part of starting something from scratch, but it's been fun for sure. And there's a lot of introspection and you have to force to cheer yourself on sometimes. Because a lot of people might think: "Oh man, being your own boss has got to be amazing."

But that's not how it works. I've got the biggest jerk boss in the world right now and it's me. I'm not going to sit here and pat myself on the back and say: "Hey, good job. Hey, take the rest of the day off." It's hard when you have certain standards.

When I talk to my class about entrepreneurship, I tell them you kind of have to learn how to do things, like doing your own stunts.

You don't have a guy to say to: "Take care of that search engine optimization and optimize that web content for me. Hey, proofread this and clean up this graphic design. I need it to be awesome." I don't have any of that. I'm doing all my own stunts from an entrepreneurial standpoint.

You have limited resources and you just have to figure it out. If you ever want to grow into some sort of leadership role, you have to know what it was like to actually do that stuff.

Bruce Lee did his own stunts. When he was Kato, he was blowing people's minds away. He took it to the next level. He changed the whole face of it.

Another thing you hear in startup land is you have to move quickly. And he famously moved so fast that the cameras back then couldn't even pick up all of his motions. So they actually had to tell him: "Slow down a little bit. We can't pick that up." But the fact that he was too fast, faster than the tech at the time, and they couldn't keep up with him is amazing. And I love how they reacted: "Wow. Okay. Not only have we not seen anyone do this before, but you're way too fast for us." And he forced the tech to speed up to keep up with him.

Being able to stay ahead of the curve is good. But greatness happens, the Bruce Lee level of greatness happens, when you're able to stay ahead of the curve and you're not just following or keeping up with something. You're blazing the trail. You're moving faster than the tech and force everyone to keep up with you.

CHAPTER 5

Be Curious, My Friend

We frequently look at successful people and think that their talent is limited to those things for which they are most famous. But high achievers often excel at more than one thing. Leonardo da Vinci painted the Mona Lisa, but he also sketched designs for a helicopter and an airplane. Thomas Jefferson wrote the Declaration of Independence, but he was also an accomplished architect. Albert Einstein was a theoretical physicist, but he was also a pretty good violin player.

In fact, research has shown that many high achievers, whether in science or business, were also accomplished in the arts. Prominent organizational psychologist Adam Grant notes:

> People who started businesses and contributed to patent applications were more likely than their peers to have leisure time hobbies that involved, drawing, painting, architecture, scuplture, and literature.[1]

One study by Michigan State University found that Nobel Prize Winners were more likely to be involved in the arts than less accomplished scientists. In fact, they found that they were twice as likely to be proficient in music (playing instruments, composing, conducting), around seven times as likely to be interested in the arts (drawing, painting, printmaking sculpting) or in crafts like woodworking or glassblowing, twelve times more likely to be writers (poets, playwrights, novelists, essayists), and as much as twenty-two times more likely to be performers (amateur actors, dancers, magicians).[2]

So it probably shouldn't surprise you that Bruce Lee participated in every category on this list. He didn't win a Nobel Prize, but his enormous curosity and willingness to stretch himself were key factors in his success. Grant explains:

> Interest in the arts among entrepreneurs, inventors, and eminent scientists obviously reflects their curiosity and aptitude. People who are open to new ways of looking at science and business also tend to be fasincated by the expression of ideas and emotions through images, sounds, and words.[3]

Growing up in Hong Kong, Lee wasn't a particularly good student. But by the time he attended the University of Washington in Seattle, he not only worked hard to improve his grades, but demonstrated an intense curiosity for all kinds of knowledge. Whether sitting by Lake Washington or at a table in his favorite restaurant, he could often be found drawing, sketching, or even writing poetry, and his fascination with verse, rhyme, and meter continued throughout his life.

Lee was a voracious reader, consuming everything from traditional Chinese picture books to works from both Eastern and Western thinkers like Carl Jung, René Descartes, Plato, Zhuang Zhou (the "founder" of Taoism), and Jiddu Krishnamurti. Books were piled throughout his house and even overflowed into his garage.

But Lee wasn't content just to consume and accept information. He questioned concepts and experimented with them to create new ideas of his own. He jotted down those ideas at all hours of the day, excitedly telling his wife and friends what he just discovered. When he found that something didn't work, he didn't complain; he tried to fix it. For example, he developed his own exercise equipment to reflect his philosophy on fighting. Remember how his character responded to O'Hara in *Enter the Dragon:* "Boards don't hit back." Lee wanted to create equipment that could mimic real combat without a human sparring partner. After all, punching-bags and dummies don't hit back either.

To increase his reaction speed, Lee created equipment that came at him in unpredictable ways and from unexpected angles. He also developed his own exercise routines that worked on specific areas of the body—for instance, increasing muscle mass around his shoulders and torso. He even came up with his own protein shakes, experimenting with ingredients like wheat germ, powdered milk, peanut butter, eggs, and brewer's yeast. Likewise, when he realized that Hong Kong kung fu movies weren't particularly good, he taught himself the craft of filmmaking, buying several books about it and learning as much as he could about behind-the-scenes techniques.

But Lee never worked in a vacuum. His intellectual curiosity, work ethic, creativity, and willingness to experiment are what made him so successful, even at things he had no experience doing. As technology executive Lee Huang pointed out:

When you're the head of an innovation program, you have to figure out how to get budgets, you have to experiment, and you have to have a diverse knowledge and skill set. And this is what I think is missing for most innovators.

You have to understand the business side, the technology side, the marketing side, the customer side, the operation side. You can't do everything, but you need to know how they all fit together. Bruce was a sponge, which is what you have to be. You just have to keep learning because half of the things you need to learn, you may not know, but you have to have that inquisitiveness to continually learn and then apply it and integrate it.

One thing Huang particularly admires about Lee, and something that probably doesn't get a lot of attention, is that he didn't just create new things and assume they worked.

Lee was always asking for feedback and demonstrating his creations to friends, family, and the general public—whether it was a new piece of exercise equipment or a new martial arts move like his one-inch punch, which he showcased at a tournament to see how audiences would react. He wanted to generate buzz. Huang marveled:

> No one had ever seen that before. Holy smoke! From a corporate perspective if you're giving demos or prototypes, you have to think of what will get the wow factor because again, depending on your organization, you may not get too many tries at it so you really want to have a good wow factor and to think through it.

UNDER THE SKY, ONE FAMILY

Perhaps the greatest factor in Bruce Lee's success was his overall humanity. He may not have been a civil-rights activist, waving signs and marching to the Lincoln Memorial with Martin Luther King Jr. But, as we have seen, he was firmly opposed to racism and bigotry in all forms, being himself of mixed-race heritage. His mother, Grace Ho, had both European and Jewish ancestry, while his wife was white, a fact that the news media highlighted when he was promoting *The Green Hornet* because of the rarity of mixed-race marriages in the United States during the 1960s.

When Pierre Berton asked Lee whether he considered himself Chinese or American, Lee said neither, replying: "You know what I want to think of myself? As a human being." Racism ran completely contrary to Lee's quest to better himself. People, he felt, should always be evolving and racism was the result of traditions and static patterns that he so clearly disliked:

> The simple truth is that these opinions on such things as racism are traditions, which are nothing more than a "formula" laid down by these elder people's experience. As we progress and time changes, it is necessary to reform this formula.[4]

Whether in Seattle, Oakland, Los Angeles, or Hong Kong, Lee made many friends from different races and backgrounds. A major part in his popularity was his willingness to teach kung fu to anyone—white, Black, female, Asian, or non-Asian. Before that, traditional Chinese believed the martial arts were exclusive to their culture and that only Chinese people should be allowed to learn them.[5]

———————————

"Under the sky, under the heaven, man, there is but one family. It just so happens that people are different."

———————————

Doug Palmer recalls the first time he met Bruce Lee:

I was [at a street fair] with friends milling around, just kind of checking out the action and I ran into a friend that I had asked about meeting Bruce. It turned out her younger brother was taking lessons from him. She had asked if I was still interested in meeting him. I said, "Sure," thinking it would be some time in the future.

And not long after that I felt a tap on my shoulder and I turned around and there was

Bruce standing there looking at me with kind of a neutral expression on his face. And he said: "I heard you were looking for me."

He said it in a way in which he thought I was looking to challenge him or something. I didn't want to crowd his space and he was standing in a way that kind of suggested he was ready for anything. So I kind of leaned with an awkward reach and stuck my hand out and introduced myself and told him I had seen his demo in Chinatown and was interested in learning from him.

He nodded and he said: "Come to the practice next week and then we'll see."

Many of Lee's relationships followed the pattern of Palmer's experience—curiosity leading to lessons, leading to friendship.

THE POWER OF DIVERSITY

Numerous studies have shown that a diverse workforce, from new employees to executives and directors, can boost a company's ability to create and innovate. The fact that white men continue to dominate the upper echelons of business in the United States may partially explain why the country's overall productivity growth is so poor despite the emergence of game-changing technologies like the Internet. As Robert Gordon of Northwestern University explains:

> We have an $18 trillion economy. Most of it is operating by the same business methods and procedures that have been in place for at least ten years. . . . In much of the economy, daily practices of business methods are not being influenced by the recent innovations in terms of robots, smartphones, or the other things that have happened more recently.[6]

Like any business, Lee's enterprises greatly benefited from him opening his social circle and exposing himself to a broad range of ideas and experiences. His close group of friends and students in Seattle included people of color—Jesse

Glover (Black), Leroy Garcia (Latino), Taky Kimura (Asian)—as well as white people like James DeMile, Ed Hart, and Skip Ellsworth.

And the same openness to diverse influences shaped all his endeavors. As biographer Matthew Polly wrote in his book *Bruce Lee: A Life:*

> Perhaps the greatest gift his students gave to Bruce was forcing him to evolve as a martial artist. When he arrived he was wedded to Chinese kung fu, convinced of its superiority. But the sheer size of Americans made him adapt. Techniques that worked in [wing chun] class were easily thwarted by opponents who were eight inches taller and a hundred pounds heavier.
>
> His students, all veteran fighters and martial artists, also introduced him to the American combat scene. From them he began to learn the value of certain judo throws and chokes and appreciate the power of Western boxing punches and fluidity of footwork. At this point, Bruce still thought of himself as a kung fu man, but he was beginning to merge the best of East and West. It was an approach that would last the rest of his

life, characterize his own art, and eventually lead to a new paradigm in the martial arts.[7]

One fascinating project that has largely escaped attention was an idea put forward by Lee and friend Jhoon Goo Rhee, a South Korean martial arts expert considered the Father of American Taekwondo, to produce a television show on teaching women self-defense tactics. In a letter to Rhee, Lee suggested several ideas, including music, sets, costumes, props, format, marketing, and merchandising:

Situation

A) Realistic duplication of actual attack (Note: whoever the attacker, he must be fierce and rough toward his victim.)

B) Provide props as much as possible to capture the street scene—like chair, phony car, etc., etc.

Lessons

1. Take one technique at a time and show it from different angles and perspectives so as not to make the lesson monotonous.

2. Needless to say, the program has to be both educational and entertaining—realize the fact that (being) too educational will make the show dull; on the other hand, too entertaining will decrease the martial art spirit. However, through a happy medium is desire, for a TV program, do lean toward showmanship.[8]

The show didn't go anywhere, but what if it had? Teaching women self-defense classes on television would have been very innovative in the 1970s.

ALWAYS COLLABORATE

As you can see, Bruce Lee was always thinking, learning, and collaborating. Even when he was gainfully employed, he was always working a "side hustle" in the belief that the project might have the potential to grow into something more significant.

In today's tech economy, where job security is almost non-existent, a person's best chance to stay relevant is essentially to emulate this. "Utimately, the most valuable asset you can possess as an employee is something that you can't neccessarily teach: curiosity," former LinkedIn executive Steve Cadigan wrote in his book *Workquake.*[9]

Cadigan lists four qualities that he believes are esssential for today's fast-changing economy:

- An appreciation of the power of experimentation
- The ability to pivot to a new career unexpectedly as life circumstances change
- Willingness to pivot to a new career path, even when at the top of a current career
- An inclination to tinker and experiment "after hours," and to find great joy and fulfillment in new ideas and oppportunities[10]

In 2014, the Copenhagen Business School in Denmark and the Munich School of Management in Germany published a study that examined 4,138 inventions from twenty-one European countries, the United States, and Japan in all major industries. The study found that inventors who continued to ponder their work outside of the office and who pursued a wide range of hobbies ultimately produced higher-quality innovations for their employers.[11]

Cadigan agrees:

> Building networks, collaborating, experimenting, and looking for opportunities in your passion projects and your hobbies are the main ingredients for you to thrive in this new world of work. Learning agility is the new superpower that will help you weather the change and uncertainty that lie before all of us.[12]

IN THE WORDS OF TONY BLAUER

Tony Blauer is founder of Blauer Tactical Systems, one of the world's leading consulting companies specializing in the research and development of performance psychology for law enforcement, the military, and corporations.

A former actor and stuntman, Blauer was also close friends with Brandon Lee, Bruce Lee's son. He describes the impact Bruce Lee had on his own personal development and his career.

In 1972, I got my ass kicked by two older teenagers. I was twelve turning thirteen. I wasn't really physically hurt, more emotionally hurt. Before they struck me one of them said, "Hey, this is what you get to look forward to when you come to high school next year." After I got jumped all I thought was, "What just happened?"

After the fight, I went home and told my dad and he said, "You need to learn how to defend yourself." At the time there was only one taekwondo school in my area, about three miles from my house, so I signed up.

It was 1973. The same year Bruce Lee died and the whole world exploded. There was this insane Bruce Lee craze. All of a sudden, he was everywhere. Then it hit me, "Hey, I know who this guy is! That's Kato, from *The Green Hornet*!" (A show I watched as a kid in the 1960s.)

I became the world's biggest Bruce Lee fan. I say that in jest because everyone thought they were. That's the power and charisma Bruce had. I was mesmerized by him. I bought every book and magazine I could. I even ordered from Hong Kong and Japan in the 1970s and had quite the collection. In fact, my whole basement was not only a gym, but also a shrine to Bruce Lee with heavy bags, training equipment, posters, pictures, and quotes all over the place. He was essentially a spiritual guide.

When I was fifteen years old, my mom asked me, "have you thought about what you're going to be when you're older? Are you going to go into the family business, become a lawyer, or a doctor?" I was on the floor trying to work on the splits, looking at a Bruce Lee magazine. And I said, "Oh mom, school's not going to be that important for me. I'm going to be a famous self-defense instructor like Bruce Lee, I'm going to teach martial arts." She patted me on the head and said, "Okay dear, we'll talk about this when you're older." But I knew. Studying Lee's mindset, grit, and resilience inspired me to believe in myself.

Bruce had that X factor. If you look at a hundred Chinese stars, athletes, like Jackie Chan, Jet Li, whomever, and then look at Bruce Lee, he had a different energy. If you had them all standing in a lineup, you'd point at him—he had something different. He didn't look like everybody else or anybody else!

I was fascinated by him as an athlete, I wanted to move like him. If you really research my system, it's truly about understanding this intersection between physiology, biomechanics, and psychology. I talk about us as "human weapon systems." When you study neurobiology and apply it, you're going to move like a human weapon.

As mentioned earlier, Bruce served as a spiritual guide. He was very philosophical. He taught people to holistically look at the big picture—mind, body, and spirit. People often ignore the mind and spirit. It might be just a fatal flaw in humans. Most don't have that self-awareness to introspect and diversify their outlook.

My favorite Lee quote is "to hell with circumstances I will create my own circumstances." That stayed with me and carried me through many dark periods.

Life is not a movie or a book. We need to create our opportunities. We need to create our leads. We need to create resilience for everything, all of the time. We all need to be inspired by Bruce's tenacity, whether for fitness, health, or relationships, that's the stuff we need to pursue every day.

Our lack of resilience and vision has a lot to do with fear. And fear is something I've struggled with all my life. I was a very good athlete, but I was always impacted by fear and self-doubt. So whenever I competed as a wrestler, skier, tennis player, whatever, I always had that trepidation, "Am I really this good? Can I really do this?" The self-doubt crippled me. I would think more about losing and failing than winning. That's what got me intrigued with martial arts and self-defense. I just somehow made this intuitive connection that if I could protect myself, then I wouldn't be afraid anymore.

This journey led me to the realization that if we can change our relationship with fear, we can change our minds. And if we can change our minds, we can potentially change our lives. The hypothesis is that fear mostly operates at an unconscious level, and quietly throttles everything we do: who we talk to therefore who we marry, who our friends are, how much money we make, what kind of job we have, and of course, whether or not we defend ourselves. All of these decisions run through our fear filter.

It's subtle and shows up differently in different people. For example, I know special ops soldiers, Tier-1 operators, who have been in gun fights with terrorists. They'll jump out of an airplane and crawl toward a building filled with the enemy—all of this takes incredible courage, but many will admit they're afraid of public speaking!

When I'm coaching, I'll make the joke: "You can be a unicorn in one part of your life and still feel like that scared seven-year-old kid in another part of your life."

It's interesting that my study of Bruce Lee has helped me grow my company and develop a system to help anyone manage fear, from the boardroom to the battlefield.

It's ironic. I remember talking to this sales group, and they weren't afraid of getting mugged or robbed. But they were afraid of not meeting their numbers and maybe losing their jobs. And that impacted how much they drank, smoked, and worried. They didn't understand how fear was running their memory system during the day and burning them out.

I actually named this mental performance system the Know Fear® program. Because getting to know fear means leaning into fear. And leaning into fear means your comfort zone grows.

In my opinion, fear management is the gateway to self-awareness. Self-awareness improves your situational awareness. If you've got good self-awareness and good situational awareness, your critical thinking skills will be activated and you will create opportunity and success just like Bruce Lee.

CHAPTER 6

Bruce Lee, Inc.

Jeff Chinn, a long-time letter carrier in San Francisco, was having lunch one day in 1993 when he glanced into his bag to see if he had dropped any crumbs on his cargo. Federal postal workers are not supposed to read their customers' mail, but something caught Chinn's eye. It was an ad in *USA Today* that read, in bold letters: Bruce Lee Auction.

His heart nearly stopped. Chinn was a superfan of Bruce Lee and had been collecting his merchandise since he was a teenager. But here was a chance to acquire something Lee had actually owned.

Chinn flew down to Beverly Hills and successfully bid $8,000 on one of the suits Lee wore in *Enter the Dragon*. Among the other items sold that day was Lee's "My Definite Chief Aim" letter, which sold for $20,000. There were also a pair of broken reading glasses, a Screen Actors Guild membership card, some canceled checks and credit card slips, and other writings and drawings.

The 1993 auction is legendary among Bruce Lee collectors today, who are legion. For one thing, Lee was only thirty-two when he died, so his estate was relatively small compared to celebrities like Elvis Presley. Lee's Hong Kong movies worked on tight budgets, which meant the costumes, sets, and props were often reused in other productions. That the auction contained as many as items as it did was mainly due to his wife Linda's natural instinct as a pack rat. As she recalls in an interview with the *Los Angeles Times*:

> In the last twenty years, there have been cycles of great interest in Bruce Lee. When he first passed away, we had no idea that he would become as legendary as he has. In agreement with both of my children, we thought that we could perhaps share [the memorabilia] with other people who might find great value in them.[1]

Demand for Bruce Lee's belongings has soared in recent years, reports Chinn, now one of the world's largest collectors.

> I think Linda and Shannon really regret that they sold all of the stuff. Because they could have used it. It's now impossible to get it back from collectors. The family did not know how the price would skyrocket. People who bought stuff at the auction and then resold it have made hundreds of times what they paid for it. It's crazy.

Chinn estimates that the suit he bought for $8,000 in 1993 is now worth well into the six figures.

But Lee's belongings and memorabilia aren't just valuable because there are so few of them, Chinn claims. What makes his brand so enduring is that Lee himself was one of a kind:

> Even though I was only twelve years old when Bruce Lee passed away, I knew in my gut that there's never going to be another one like him. Sometimes when you tell a young person to watch an old movie, they think: "Boy, this is sure

outdated. Or not impressive." But when you see Bruce Lee in his movies, there's no one that ever did it like that.

The fact is, his movies are still fresh, his philosophies are still fresh, he's the only Asian-American out there that's still relevant.

THE DRAGON ENDURES

Five decades later, Bruce Lee is still relevant. You can find him on T-shirts worn by characters in films ranging from *Superbad* and *Step Brothers* to *Avengers: Age of Ultron*. A picture of him turns up on a wall in a scene from *Seinfeld,* and footage from his films appears in a fight sequence in the movie *Limitless.* You can see his influence on NBA star Steph Curry's yellow-and-black sneakers. He looms large in the music of groups like hip-hop legend Wu Tang Clan and K-pop superstar BTS. Whenever you play *Mortal Kombat* or *Street Fighter* on your X-Box, Nintendo, or PlayStation, you can thank Bruce Lee. Whether in high-brow fare like *Crouching Tiger, Hidden Dragon* or mass entertainment like *Star Wars*, Bruce Lee looms large.

It's impossible to put a value on this—although some have tried.

A 2009 article in the *Wall Street Journal* reported that Bruce Lee Enterprises generates about $1 million a year in licensing deals, although Shannon Lee felt she could squeeze another $5 to $10 million from them.[2] The same piece quoted an expert who estimated that Lee's image is potentially worth seven figures annually. "He's truly a global icon, and there aren't many of those around," the expert said. While there are thirty or forty such personalities who really resonate in the United States, he adds, internationally the list shrinks to just a handful, including Michael Jackson, Muhammad Ali, and Bruce Lee.

When developing his films, his television shows, his martial arts schools, and his JKD philosophy, Bruce Lee always thought carefully about his brand—which makes perfect sense, since he took such a hands-on approach to his projects. The word "Dragon" in the titles of the films *Way of the Dragon* and *Enter the Dragon* refers, not to a character or plot point in the story, but rather to Lee's nickname. To Lee, the movies were personal statements that signaled his emergence as a major movie star. Can you imagine any movie star today being able to name a movie after himself or herself?

Lee clashed with Warner Bros. over the title of *Enter the Dragon*. The studio, which wanted to name the movie *Blood and Steel*, claimed the title sounded like a monster movie. But Lee persisted and eventually won out. "In retrospect, I can't imagine it being called anything else," said producer Fred Weintrub. "As a former ad man, I should have recognized the value of branding in the first place."[3] But Lee never lost sight of the importance of merchandising. Kato, the most popular character from *The Green Hornet*, still drives a robust market for all kinds of branded merchandise, from action figures, to toys, to lunch boxes.

After Lee completed *Enter the Dragon*, he instructed his lawyer Adrian Marshall to start exploring merchandising opportunities, referring to possible deals with animation studio Hanna Barbera and Warner Bros. "Also, I would like to meet with you first before meeting with Raymond Chow and then both of us will hear him out," Lee wrote to his attorney. "By the way, there are also propositions of books, clothing, endorsements, etc."[4]

One of the most amazing things about Bruce Lee is that he built his brand from nothing. Recall the teenager who, newly arrived in the United States, began telling anyone who would listen how he wanted to do big things, although the odds of him actually accomplishing them were discouragingly low, especially at a time when America was so racially polarized.

Today, almost anyone can become rich and famous by cultivating personal brands on social-media platforms. But the Internet did not exist in Lee's lifetime. He became a superstar by sheer force of will. Asked to imagine what might have been if Bruce Lee had had access to the social-media platforms available today, Steve Cadigan exclaimed:

Oh my God, his audience and followers would be off the charts. I mean, he'd be everywhere. He had charisma. He had the X-factor. He had something that, even today, lives on during an era of short attention spans and sugar-high entertainment.

BROTHER FROM ANOTHER MOTHER

A key element to Lee's powerful brand is his relationship with African-Americans. He was close friends with people like Jesse Glover and NBA legend Kareem Abdul-Jabbar, who appeared in *Game of Death.* Moreover, Lee's films, which typically centered on themes of the oppressed fighting against the oppressor, struck a resonant chord with Black audiences, who could certainly relate to the idea of oppression, having suffered the horrors of slavery, Jim Crow, and segregation.

In *Enter the Dragon*, the character Williams, played by African-American actor Jim Kelly, is accosted by racist cops when he leaves his dojo. Williams not only beats up the cops, but steals their squad car. The sequence really had nothing to do with the movie's overall plot, but you can imagine how it thrilled Black Americans who had suffered from police brutality.

Similar themes are struck in *Fist of Fury*, which takes place during the 1930s, when Japan occupied Shanghai. The Japanese conquest of China prior to and during World War II remains a source of deep humiliation and anger for the Chinese people. Thus the film, released in 1972, appealed to Chinese nationalism and the broader popular movement against colonialism. The Vietnam War was also raging at the time, a conflict that Americans saw as a battle against communism, but the Chinese saw as a war to liberate the country from Western imperialists.

One scene from *Fist of Fury* was particuarly resonant for African-Americans. In it, a guard denies Chen Zhen, played by Lee, entry to a park, noting a sign that reads: "No Dogs and Chinese Allowed." Zhen proceeds to smash the sign and beat up the Japanese men who are taunting him. As author and pop-culture critic David Walker points out in his book *Becoming Black:*

This sign, of course, recalls the "Whites Only" and "No Blacks Allowed" signs found through various parts of the United States just a few years earlier. The sting of humiliation born out of exclusion, the soul-crushing dehumanization felt by the oppressed, proved to be so universal that it transcended nationality and culture.

Black audiences in America understood the "No Dogs and Chinese Allowed" sign in a way that eluded most white audiences—its message resonating on a level that seemed to tell us we were not alone in a world that did not want us.

And so, Chen Zhen became an iconic hero of the oppressed. The fact that he was discriminated against for his race made him have even more in common with Black audiences.

> *"Those who are unaware*
> *they are walking in darkness*
> *will never seek the light."*

Through Lee, Black Americans got to live out a fantasy of not only taking revenge against an oppressor, but of doing so through an exciting action form in martial arts. Cops may have badges, batons, and guns, but martial arts empowered the oppressed to fight back with hands, feet, and deep wisdom.

Warrior actor Perry Yung, who grew up near Chinatown in Oakland, California, recalls how Bruce Lee films helped Asian-Americans gain new respect from Black people.

When Bruce Lee movies came out, all those downtown theaters were suddenly showing *Return of the Dragon* and *Enter the Dragon*, $3 and $4 matinees, and stuff like that. We'd see lines around the block of Black people wearing kung fu outfits and karate outfits. Suddenly, we weren't getting picked on any more. As we walked down the line, we'd get high-fives from these older Black guys. That didn't happen before Bruce Lee. It was more like: "Give us your lunch money."

And after Bruce Lee, it was more like: "Oh, you know that martial arts stuff? Show us some of that stuff." It was a very exciting new wave form that was coming out, this empowering martial arts, based on the individual self. I wasn't the only one affected by it. It was the Black community who also needed a role model that was not white, versus what was usually offered to us from Hollywood.

Lee's work helped to encourage African-American cultural innovations like break dancing, which resembled the kinetic movements of martial arts fighting, and hip-hop and rap music, with its focus on Black Americans rebelling against systematic racism and oppression. "Bruce Lee melded so many different styles of martial arts with moves from Muhammad Ali, philosophies from Taoism and Buddhism, but he was also conscious of [people like] Malcolm X and the struggle of Black America," said RZA, one of the members of the group Wu Tang Clan. "It shows up all in his work and his persona."

Those films together were pivotal sources of inspirations for me. Think about it. In *Enter the Dragon*, there's an incorporation of the white karate guy with John Saxon, the Black martial arts brother with Jim Kelly, and Asian with Bruce Lee. They were all working together against the oppressor who was poisoning the people. If you add in a few other elements, that's our country, bro![5]

SUPER BRUCE

Lee's films ignited a kung fu craze that rapidly spread throughout America in the 1970s and helped launched blockbuster franchises in comic books, video games, and cinema in the decades that followed.

Stan Lee, the legendary comic book artist at Marvel, was certainly a Bruce Lee fan. Unlike characters like Iron Man, the Hulk, Thor, and Captain America, Bruce Lee did not have any super powers or supernatural abilities and used no advanced technology. He used intelligence and physical skills to defeat his enemies. In fact, what made him special was the fact that he was a human who did extraordinary things. As Stan Lee said: "He was believable, he was a superhero, but the attraction was that he was *real*. You felt like you could be him."

> Bruce Lee was a man of peace, he was a man of philosophy, he encouraged people to be the best they could be. He wasn't violent. In fact, that was the similarity between Bruce and many of the characters at Marvel. They weren't looking for a fight, they did their best not to get into fights.[6]

In 1973, shortly after *Enter the Dragon* debuted in the United States, Marvel published *The Hands of Shang-Chi: Master of Kung Fu* and then followed up with *The Deadly Hands of Kung Fu*, which paid direct homage to Bruce Lee. In 2021, Disney, which had acquired Marvel, released *Shang-Chi: The Legend of the Ten Rings*. The critically acclaimed film, starring Simu Liu, ultimately grossed $432.2 million in global box office.

Bruce Lee also wielded enormous influence over one of the most successful comic book characters of all time—Batman. Lee's connection to Batman dates all the way back to *The Green Hornet*, a series William Dozier created to exploit the success of the *Batman* television show. In that series, Adam West starred as a campy character who used fancy gadgets and vehicles to help police fight crime.

But in the early 1970s, at the peak of Bruce Lee's career, Dennis O'Neil and Neal Adams rewrote Batman as a darker, brooding character and played up his martial arts background. In one comic book, Batman/Bruce Wayne is shown to be proficient at jeet kune do. Another issue has him battling Bruce Lee himself. This grittier, fight-focused take on the caped crusader informed filmmaker Christopher Nolan's blockbuster movie triology: *Batman Begins*, *The Dark Knight*, and *The Dark Knight Rises*. Together, these movies grossed $2.4 billion worldwide.

Bruce Lee's success, of course, paved the way for other action stars like Jet Li, Jackie Chan, Steven Segal, Chuck Norris, and Jason Statham to star in popcorn entertainment. But Lee's effort to elevate the artistic excellence of the genre also directly influenced more thoughtful, higher-brow work that attracted both box office success and critical acclaim—witness *Crouching Tiger, Hidden Dragon*, which won an Oscar for Best Foreign Film.

This movie, directed by Ang Lee, was inspired by the martial arts fantasy stories of ancient China, a genre known as *wuxia*. But Ang Lee took great care to make sure that the elaborately staged fight scenes said something meaningful about Chinese culture and the relationships between people. Sound familiar? Ang Lee underscored the importance of this:

> Chinese martial arts are not just martial arts. It's a way of life, it's philosophy, it's how humans relate to nature. I really wanted to project that into the drama and everything in the movie.
>
> When people fight, I treat it like a conversation, like a verbal drama. There's a relationship, a development going on, there's conflict.[7]

Despite subtitles, *Crouching Tiger, Hidden Dragon* generated $213.5 million in global box office sales.

Bruce Lee's infusion of big philosphical ideas into martial arts films can also be seen in two Keanu Reeves–led blockbuster franchises: *The Matrix* and

John Wick. In the former, Neo, Reeves's character, uses martial arts, especially kung fu, to fight back against the efforts of sentient machines to control humans through an elaborate computer program. Reeves even pays homage to Lee by mimicking two of his trademark moves: he rubbed his nose with his thumb and he left his leg extended mid-air after a side kick. The four films, which collectively grossed $1.8 billion, posed thought-provoking questions about freedom, reality, and free will.

In *John Wick,* Reeves plays a retired, widowed hit man who resumes his career with tragic consequences. The films explore violence and its impact on the soul. Again, Reeves nods to Bruce Lee in one film when he fights the bad guys in a room full of mirrors, just as Lee did in *Enter the Dragon.* The *John Wick* films generated $573 million.

FATHER OF MMA

Two men, each wearing what looks like miniture boxing gloves, face each other. As they start to fight, each throws a variety of kicks and punches.

Finally, one fighter gets the better of the other with a pair of judo-like throws, before bringing his opponent to the ground with an arm bar. Writhing in pain, the defeated fighter taps out. Sounds like a mixed martial arts bout from the Ultimate Fighting Championship (UFC), doesn't it? In reality, however, the fight, which features Bruce Lee and Sammo Hung, is from the first scene of *Enter the Dragon*, a film that predates the UFC by twenty years.

Lee's innovations in that one scene alone, from the gloves to the synthesis of grappling and striking, is not lost on the fighters and executives who populate the UFC, one of the world's most popular and valuable sports franchises. "He was way ahead of his time," former UFC light heavyweight champion Tito Ortiz acknowledges. "He was doing things back then that we are doing now. Bruce Lee was the first fighter of mixed martial arts."[8]

In truth, Bruce Lee did not like structured martial arts tournaments, so he probably would not have competed in the UFC. Nevertheless, he recognized the strategic value of using multiple martial arts techniques to fight an opponent, a philosophy that forms the heart of jeet kune do.

> *"Man, the living creature, the creating individual, is always more important than any established style or system."*

"If you look at the way Bruce Lee trained, the way he fought, and many of the things he wrote, he said the perfect style was no style," said UFC president Dana White, who called Lee the Father of MMA. "You take a little something from everything. You take the good things from every different discipline, use what works, and you throw the rest away."[9] And judging by the scene from *Enter the Dragon* described above, Lee also knew that deploying different martial arts in one fight just made for exciting entertainment.

Today, the UFC is one of the world's most valuable and popular sports leagues, especially among younger people. UFC events are broadcast to over 165 countries and territories, and watched by more than 1.1 billion television households worldwide in over forty different languages. About 40 percent of UFC's viewers are between the ages of eighteen and thirty-four, the highest concentration of millennials and Gen Z of any sports audience.[10] In 2019, the UFC signed a five-year deal with ESPN worth $750 million.[11] The league is now estimated to be worth $9 to $10 billion, making it more valuable than the National Hockey League, the English Premiere League, and the National Basketball League.[12]

Many of the UFC's most popular fighters say they emulate Bruce Lee. "I look at the opponent," former UFC lightweight and welterweight champion Conor McGregor told Tony Robbins. "I look, you know. Know yourself to know others. That's a Bruce Lee quote. If you truly know yourself, you can know others."[13]

Former UFC heavyweight champion Randy Couture also acknowledges Lee's impact on the sport:

I don't know a kid who didn't watch Bruce Lee movies and afterward got a pair of nunchaku and started to twirl them around. I thought Bruce Lee was the "man" when I was kid. He's definitely someone I admired.

As a martial artist, he stressed keeping an open mind and allowing for individual style, and not getting caught up in traditional trappings, which limits some of the traditional styles. The way of his thinking was that everybody can learn from him, not just martial artists.[14]

BRUCE LEE, WARRIOR

Perhaps the greatest testament to Bruce Lee's enduring appeal is that his ideas and projects seem consistently to find new life. *Warrior*, a series that so far has enjoyed three seasons and is currently streaming on HBO Max, originated from the idea of the American Western kung fu series that Lee had unsuccessfully pitched to Warner Bros. in 1971.

In *Warrior*, Shannon Lee and *Fast and Furious: Tokyo Drift* director Justin Lin teamed up to tell the story of Ah Sahm, a Chinese immigrant with extraordinary martial arts skills, who travels to San Francisco during the 1870s in search of his sister. He soon gets embroiled in the Tong Wars, a battle among rival gangs to control Chinatown. Shannon Lee, who worked as executive producer on the film, comments on its personal significance:

> My father specifically wanted to set the show during this time. My father was very focused on telling Chinese stories, and this is a Chinese-American story that takes place during two significant, true cultural, historical events, which are the Tong Wars of San Francisco's Chinatown and the Chinese Exclusion Act. So, while those things were in his notes, and in various drafts of the treatment, we wanted to make sure we really developed that out, and those tensions were really present in the drama of the show.[15]

Warrior embodies Bruce Lee's artistic ambitions, a fusion of high kinetic action, historically rich drama, multi-dimensional characters, and the complicated relationship between East and West.

Moreover, the series tackles heady subjects like immigration, racism, and economic competition through the eyes of Asian-Americans, a group Hollywood had long marginalized.

Lee's daughter goes on to explain:

Our goal is always to play within the realm that we are in. We have a lot of Old West tropes and Kung Fu movie tropes, and things that we can play with, but at the same time, we want to subvert the expectations. We want our characters to be rich, deep, fully human and flawed, but also powerful, in their own right.[16]

And that was Bruce Lee's goal all along.

CONCLUSION: WHAT IF?

Bruce Lee's resumé is actually quite thin on paper. He starred in only five films, one of which, *Game of Death*, was not even completed in his lifetime. You can count on one hand the number of television shows in which he appeared. The same goes for the martial arts schools he opened.

Yet he remains a global superstar, his influence and impact undiminished over the fifty years since his tragic death at the age of thirty-two. Perhaps that's why Lee continues to fascinate people. He accomplished so much in such a short lifetime.

Which begs the question I'm sure lots of people have pondered: What if Bruce Lee hadn't died? What if he were still alive today?

It would be a safe bet that Lee would have continued to make movies. People consider *Enter the*

Dragon his masterpiece, but Lee was hardly satisfied with it, or with any movie he made before that. His acting was always a work in progress and he was obsessed with quality.

"There are no limits. There are only plateaus, and you must not stay there, you must go beyond them."

One interesting question is whether Lee would have transcended the martial arts genre. No other actor of Asian descent who broke into stardom with martial arts films—whether Jackie Chan, Michelle Yeoh, Donnie Yen, Jet Li, or Simu Liu—has been able to make commercially and critically successful films without throwing a kick or a punch. Could Lee have done Shakespeare? Or a romantic comedy? Or perhaps a neo-noir murder mystery? Would he even have wanted to? We'll never know.

But given his entrepreneurial instincts, Lee would certainly have been active in the film industry as a producer, a director, or a studio head. He already owned a production company in Concord Pictures and was exploring merchandising deals.

It would also be fascinating to see how Lee might have used today's technology—social media or streaming services—to build his brand. Can you imagine a Bruce Lee YouTube channel or Instagram page? How about exclusive development deals with Netflix, Hulu, or Apple TV?

Given his penchant for fashion and style, Lee might have launched his own clothing and accessories business. Perhaps a collaboration with Target or H&M? Or limited-edition sneakers sold exclusively through Foot Locker? He was also interested in music. Perhaps Little Dragon Studios might have produced promising hip-hop artists.

Bruce Lee was not overtly political nor particularly vocal about social issues. As Lee was still building his career, he preferred to lead by example. But, if he were alive today and financially secure, would he have used his platform and influence to take a more active stance against racism and discrimination, especially against Asian-Americans? Or would he have used his power to open the doors for more people of color to find opportunities in Hollywood?

Questions like these make us realize just how much we lost when Bruce Lee died so tragically at such a young age. And yet we can be thankful for all he accomplished in his short life, and for the enduring impact he continues to exert on people worldwide.

"The key to immortality is first living a life worth remembering."

BIBILIOGRAPHY

Cadigan, Steve. *Workquake: Embracing the Aftershocks of Covid-19 to Create a Better Model of Working.* Herdon, Virgina: Amplify Publishing, 2021.

Grant, Adam. *Originals: How Non-Comformists Move the World.* New York: Penguin Books, 2017.

Kerridge, Steve and Darren Chua. *Bruce Lee: The Intercepting Fist.* London: On The Fly Productions, 2020.

Lee, Linda. *The Life and Tragic Death of Bruce Lee.* London: W. H. Allen & Company, 1975.

Lee, Shannon. *Be Water, My Friend: The Teachings of Bruce Lee.* New York: Flatiron Books, 2021.

Little, John. *Bruce Lee: Letters from the Dragon.* Hong Kong: Tuttle Publishing, 2016.

Polly, Matthew. *Bruce Lee: A Life.* New York: Simon & Schuster, 2019.

Rafiq, Fiaz. *Bruce Lee: Life of a Legend.* Edinburgh: Arena Sport, 2020.

Walker, David F. *Becoming Black: Personal Ramblings on Racial Identification, Racism, and Popular Culture.* Portland, Oregon: Drapetomedia, 2013.

ENDNOTES

Preface

1. Associated Press, "More Than 9,000 Anti-Asian Incidents Have Been Reported Since the Pandemic Began," *National Public Radio* (Last modified August 12, 2021), *www.npr.org.*

2. Shannon Lee, *Be Water, My Friend: The Teachings of Bruce Lee* (New York: Flatiron Books, 2020), 5.

3. Ibid.

Introduction

1. John Little, *Bruce Lee: Letters of the Dragon* (Hong Kong: Tuttle Publishing, 2016), 25.

2. "Letter to Pearl," podcast #120, *brucelee.com.*

3. Ibid.

4. Michelle Jamrisko, Wei Lu, and Alexandre Tanzi, "South Korea Leads World in Innovation as U.S. Exits Top Ten," *Bloomberg News* (Last modified February 3, 2021), *www.bloomberg.com.*

5. Jill Young Miller, "Knot Wins Olin Award for Research Quotient Paper," Washington University in St. Louis, Olin blog, *olinblog.wustl.edu.*

6. Mark Perry, "Stunning College Degree Gap: Women Have Earned Almost 10 Million More College Degrees than Men Since 1982," *American Enterprise Institute* (May 13, 2013), *www.aei.org.*

7. Amanda Weinstein. "When More Women Join the Workforce, Wages Rise—Including for Men." *Harvard Business Review* (January 31, 2018), *hbr.org.*

8. Daniel Sandberg, "When Women Lead, Firms Win," S&P Global (October 16, 2019), *www.spglobal.com.*

9. Michael D. Sheer and Miriam Jordan, "Trump Suspends Visas Allowing Hundreds of Thousands of Foreigners to Work in the United States." *New York Times* (Last modified July 23, 2020), *www.nytimes.com.*

10. Pew Research Center, "Trust in America: How Do Americans View Economic Inequality?" *www.pewresearch.org.*

11. Katherine Schaeffer, "A Growing Share of Americans Say Affordable Housing Is a Big Problem Where They Live," Pew Research Center (January 18, 2022), *www.pewresearch.org.*

12. Bill Whitaker, "The Great Resignations: Why More Americans Are Quitting Their Jobs than Ever Before," CBS News (January 9, 2022), *www.cbsnews.com.*

13. Robert Sobel, "Essays, Papers, and Addresses: Coolidge and American Business," Calvin Coolidge Presidential Foundation, *coolidgefoundation.org.*

14. Ibid.

15. "Letter to Pearl," podcast #120, *brucelee.com.*

Chapter 2

1. Eve Zibart, "The Lennon Sound," Washington Post (December 10, 1980), *www.washingtonpost.com.*

2. David Bennett, "How Much Music Theory Did the Beatles Know?" *www.youtube.com.*

3. Mike Cane, "Steve Jobs Insult Response," *www.you tube.com.*

4. Ibid.

5. Linda Lee, *The Life and Tragic Death of Bruce Lee* (London: W. H. Allen & Company, 1975), 60.

6. "Letter to Pearl," podcast #120, *brucelee.com.*

7. Ibid. Lee's letter to Pearl is remarkable in that he clearly states his vision/mission in life at an age when most of us are more preoccupied with dating and finding a job. Bruce clearly invested a lot of thought into the letter; he actually went through many drafts before sending it off—almost as if he were aware that he was creating something important for posterity beyond writing to a friend.

8. Linda Lee, *The Life and Tragic Death of Bruce Lee,* 10.

9. Bruce Lee Interview (Pierre Berton Show, 1971), *www.youtube.com.*

10. Jonathan Woetzel, Jeongmin Seong, Nick Leung, et al., "China and the World: Inside the Dynamics of a Changing Relationship," McKinsey Global Institute, *www.mckinsey.com.*

11. Travis Clark, "China Has Surpassed the U.S. as the World's Biggest Box Office. Here's the Government's 5-Year Plan for Its Movie Industry," *Business Insider* (November 18, 2021), *www.businessinsider.in.*

12. Terry Gross, "Hollywood Relies on China to Stay Afloat. What Does This Mean for Movies?" *National Public Radio* (February 21, 2022), *www.npr.org.*

13. "Letter to Pearl," podcast #120, *brucelee.com.*

14. Linda Lee, *The Life and Tragic Death of Bruce Lee,* 75.

15. "'My Definite Chief Aim': Bruce Lee's Letter to Himself," Angry Asian Man blog, *blog.angryasian man.com.*

16. Steve Kerridge and Darren Chua, *Bruce Lee: The Intercepting Fist* (London: On The Fly Productions, 2020).

Chapter 3

1. Robert C.Barkman, "Why the Human Brain Is so Good at Detecting Patterns," *Psychology Today* (May 19, 2021), *www.psychologytoday.com.*

2. Thomas Lee, "What's Up with Those British Red Telephone Booths?" *Star Tribune* (July 19, 2013), *www.startribune.com.*

3. Thomas Lee, "Valuation, Not Regulation, Is What Held Silicon Valley IPOs Back," *San Francisco Chronicle* (April 22, 2017), *www.sfchronicle.com.*

4. "Obstacles in the Way," podcast #107, *brucelee.com.*

5. "Reform the Formula," podcast #75, *brucelee.com.*

6. "Broken Rhythm," podcast #90, *brucelee.com.*

7. Ibid.

8. Paul Graham, "Ideas for Startups," in Essays, *www .paulgraham.com.*

9. Steve Jobs, "Introducing the New iPhone PART 1," *www.youtube.com.*

10. John Little, *Bruce Lee: Letters of the* Dragon, 77.

11. *Iron Fists and Kung Fu Kicks.* Directed by Serge Ou, performance by Jessica Hardwick, Scott Adkins, Michael Jai White. Widebear Entertainment, 2019. Netflix.

12. Ibid.

13. Ibid.

14. Ibid.

15. One of Lee's often-overlooked innovations from Hollywood was having someone score original music for his films rather than using the canned music that was prevelant in kung fu cinema. For *Way of the Dragon*, Lee even played a percussion instrument during one of the recording sessions.

16. Linda Lee, *The Life and Tragic Death of Bruce Lee*, 148.

17. Hong Kong kung fu cinema has produced some of the world's best stuntmen and fight choreographers, including Tsui Hark, Andrew Lau, and Yuen Woo-ping. Some, like Donnie Yen, Jackie Chan, and Sammo Hung, followed Lee's path and found success in Hollywood.

18. Linda Lee, *The Life and Tragic Death of Bruce Lee,* 149.

19. In real life, Lee was a devoted athelete and trained as such. He developed countless exercises to stretch and

warm up, knowing flexibility depended on joints and the elasticity and firmness of the ligaments, as well as the condition of the cartilage and tendons.

20. Bruce Lee Interview (Pierre Berton Show, 1971), *www.youtube.com.*

21. Wayne Wong, "Nothingness in Motion: Theorizing Bruce Lee's Action Aesthetics." *Global Media and China*, 4, no. 3 (2019).

22. I compiled these figures from a number of sources, including Box Office Mojo, Wikipedia, and IMDb. I also adjusted for inflation using April 2022 dollars.

Chapter 4

1. Thomas Lee, "How John Sculley and Steve Jobs Hated and Helped Each Other," *San Francisco Chronicle* (Last updated October 10, 2014), *www.sfgate.com.*

2. Matthew Polly, *Bruce Lee: A Life* (New York: Simon & Schuster Paperbacks, 2018), 193.

3. Steve Kerridge and Darren Chua, *Bruce Lee: The Intercepting Fist.*

4. Ibid.

5. Ibid.

6. USC Annenberg, "Annenberg Inclusion Initiative Releases Study of Representation in Netflix Original Productions," *annenberg.usc.edu.*

7. Shannon Lee, *Be Water, My Friend*, ix.

8. Ibid., 24.

9. Bruce Lee Interview (Pierre Berton Show, 1971), *www.youtube.com.*

10. John Little, *Bruce Lee: Letters of the Dragon*, 162.

11. Linda Lee, *The Life and Tragic Death of Bruce Lee*, 134.

12. Ibid., 147.

13. One notable exception was Bryna Productions. The production company, founded by actor Kirk Douglas in 1949, was behind major commercial and critical hits like *Paths of Glory, Spartacus*, and *One Flew Over the Cuckoo's Nest.*

14. Steve Kerridge, Darren Chua, *Bruce Lee: The Intercepting Fist.*

15. Matthew Polly, *Bruce Lee: A Life,* 292.

16. Linda Lee, *The Life and Tragic Death of Bruce Lee,* 119, 158.

17. John Little, *Bruce Lee: Letters of the Dragon,* 165–166.

18. This letter, dated March 28, 1972, was part of group of previously unseen documents the Bruce Lee Foundation lent to the *We Are Bruce Lee* exhibit in San Francisco.

19. Ibid.

Chapter 5

1. Adam Grant, *Originals: How Non-Comformists Move the World* (New York: Penguin Books, 2017), 47.

2. Ibid., 46.

3. Ibid., 47

4. Bruce Lee Interview (Pierre Berton Show, 1971), *www.youtube.com*.

5. This tension led to Lee's famous 1964 bout with kung fu master Wong Jack-man in Oakland. According to Linda Lee, the San Francisco Chinatown community recruited Jack-man to challenge Lee to duel. If Lee lost, he would stop teaching kung fu to white people. Linda Lee said her husband handily defeated Jack-man but some witnesses claim the duel was a draw.

6. As quoted by Adam Chandler, "Why Are Americans Getting Less Productive?" *The Atlantic Monthly* (August 12, 2016), *www.theatlantic.com*.

7. Matthew Polly, *Bruce Lee: A Life*, 100.

8. John Little, *Bruce Lee: Letters of the Dragon*, 131.

9. Steve Cadigan, *Workquake: Embracing the Aftershocks of Covid-19 to Create a Better Model of Working* (Herdon, Virgina: Amplify Publishing, 2021), 58.

10. Ibid, 74.

11. Lee N. Davis, Jerome Davis, and Karin Hoisl, "What Inspires Leisure Time Invention?" (January 2009), LMU Munich, *epub.ub.uni-muenchen.de*.

12. Steve Cadigan, *Workquake*, 92.

Chapter 6

1. Monica Yant, "Bruce Lee Items to Go on the Block," *Los Angeles Times* (July 19, 1993), *www.latimes.com*.

2. Sarah McBride, "Battling to Make Bruce Lee a Lucrative Brand," *Wall Street Journal* (October 23, 2009), *www.wsj.com.*

3. Matthew Polly, *Bruce Lee: A Life*, 421.

4. John Little, *Bruce Lee: Letters of the Dragon*, 183. The letter, dated July 20, 1973, is the last one Lee ever wrote. Marshall received it seven days after he died.

5. Justin Tinsley, "Wu-Tang's RZA on the Influence of Bruce Lee," Andscape website (June 5, 2020), *and scape.com.*

6. Kourtnee Jackson, "How Bruce Lee and His Son Were Connected to the Marvel Superhero Universe," *Showbiz Cheat Sheet* (May 31, 2020), *www.cheatsheet .com.*

7. Tyler Aquilina, "Ang Lee Reflects on *Crouching Tiger, Hidden Dragon* 20 Years Later," *Entertainment Weekly, ew.com.*

8. Fiaz Rafiq, *Bruce Lee: Life of a Legend* (Edinburgh: Arena Sport, 2020), 341.

9. Douglas Parkes, "Is Bruce Lee Really the 'Father of Mixed Martia Arts?' UFC President Dana White Thinks So—but Is He Right?" *South China Morning Post* (July 20, 2020), *www.scmp.com.*

10. "The Brand: History of UFC," UFC website, *www .ufc.com.*

11. Michael Tedder, "Did Disney's ESPN Make a Deal that Threatens Endeavor's UFC?" *TheStreet* (January 26, 2022), *www.thestreet.com.*

12. Sapphires Sealey, "Net Worth: How Much Is the UFC Worth?" Fansided website, *fansided.com.*

13. Aashish Kumar, "Former UFC Champion Conor McGregor Reveals His Trash-Talk Game Stems from Bruce Lee," *Essentially Sports* (March 17, 2022), *www .essentiallysports.com.*

14. Fiaz Rafiq, *Bruce Lee: Life of a Legend,* 340.

15. Michael Hein, "Warrior: Bruce Lee's Daughter Shannon Reveals How His Original Writings Inspired the Series," *Pop Culture* (January 20, 2021), *popculture.com.*

16. Christina Radish, "Shannon Lee on *Warrior,* Season 2, and Her Father Bruce Lee's legacy," *Collider* (May 3, 2019), *collider.com.*

ABOUT THE AUTHOR

Thomas Lee is a long-time business journalist and author of *Rebuilding Empires: How Best Buy and Other Retailers Are Transforming and Competing in the Digital Age of Retailing* (St. Martin's Press).

Lee was a business columnist for the *San Francisco Chronicle* and a business reporter for the *Star Tribune* in Minneapolis and the *St. Louis Post-Dispatch*. He is the receipient of the 2014 Gerald Loeb Award for Distinguished Business and Financial Journalism, the highest honor in his field.

Lee served as the lead curator and editorial director for the *We Are Bruce Lee* exhibit at the Chinese Historical Society of America museum in San Francisco's Chinatown. A native of Boston, he currently resides in the Bay Area.